THE
PEACEABLE REVOLUTION

THE

PEACEABLE

BY BETTY SCHECHTER

REVOLUTION

Houghton Mifflin Company Boston / / The Riverside Press Cambridge

7021

ACKNOWLEDGMENTS

THE AUTHOR wishes to thank the following publishers for permission to include the quotations listed below:

The John Day Company, Inc. for the quotations on pages 97 and 115 from TOWARD FREEDOM by Jawaharlal Nehru, copyright 1941.

Harper & Brothers for the quotations on pages 80, 110, and 113 from THE LIFE OF MAHATMA GANDHI by Louis Fischer, copyright 1950, and for the quotations on pages 153, 157, 158, 176, 177, 184 and 185 from STRIDE TOWARD FREEDOM by Martin Luther King, Jr., copyright 1958.

Houghton Mifflin Company for the quotations on pages 132, 134 and 135 from THE HINGE OF FATE by Winston S. Churchill, copyright 1950.

Alfred A. Knopf, Inc. for the quotations on page 98 from PRISON AND CHOCOLATE CAKE by Nayantara Sahgal, copyright 1954, and for the quotation on page 197 from THE SELECTED POEMS OF LANGSTON HUGHES, copyright 1959.

Public Affairs Press for the quotations on pages 75 and 77 from GANDHI'S AUTOBIOGRAPHY, copyright 1948.

G. P. Putnam's Sons for the quotation on page 97 from A KING'S STORY: The Memoirs of the Duke of Windsor, copyright 1947, 1950, 1951.

Simon & Schuster, Inc. for the quotations on pages 117 and 118 from I FOUND NO PEACE by Webb Miller, copyright 1937.

C O N T E N T S

III THE AMERICAN NEGROES

To Edward Schechter

Preface

HAS MAN'S POWER to destroy outpaced his capacity to do good?
This has come to be the dominant question of our time. Though
many people, preoccupied with the balance of power and the
threat of ultimate violence, see the answer as a disheartening
"yes" there is a growing body of evidence pointing to another
answer. *The Peaceable Revolution* is an important part of that
evidence.

Peaceable Revolution. The words seem to contradict each
other. Historically, revolutions have been violent, bloody up-
risings of people who, believing themselves wronged, united and
by the force of arms attempted to change the order of things.
Where their physical strength was greater than that of their opponents their revolts succeeded; where they were weak they were
crushed. Until recent times this has been the immutable nature
of revolt. Might has inevitably made right.

In the twentieth century, however, another kind of revolution
has been fought. Attacks have been launched and battles won
by men and women whose most powerful weapon was the conscience of their opponents. Militant in their determination to
win, they have, nonetheless, refused to resort to violence; hating
not their oppressors but their oppression, they have sought not
conquest but reconciliation. Theirs have been peaceable revolts
based on the idea and the method of nonviolent resistance to evil.

This is the story of three phases of the Peaceable Revolution:
of Henry Thoreau and his lonely rebellion in Concord, Massachusetts; of Mohandas Gandhi who dared to stand unarmed against
the might of an empire; of the American Negroes of today who
are presenting their country with one of its greatest challenges.
White man, brown man, black men. The magic of an idea bridges
the vast reaches of time and space and custom that separate
them. In the history of man's unending quest for justice they
point the way to a new method of protest, an effective method
and a bloodless one.

It may be that modern man, living in the shadow of his terrible
weapons of destruction, can find in the nonviolence of Thoreau,
Gandhi and the American Negroes one of the paths leading out
into the light.

THE
PEACEABLE REVOLUTION

I

Henry David Thoreau

1

The Making of a Rebel

ONE DAY in July, 1846, Henry Thoreau was arrested and put in jail. Within an hour after the cell door had clanged shut behind him, everybody in Concord, Massachusetts, had heard about it.

Whatever had Henry done? Refused to pay his tax. Maybe he didn't have the money. No, it wasn't the money. He'd said that his conscience wouldn't let him pay, that he was doing his duty as a citizen by refusing. Oh, that. Henry always had some mighty strange ideas about what his duty was. They'd made him kind of eccentric. Yes, but being eccentric off there in the woods by himself was one thing and mixing with the State of Massachusetts was another. It was funny how those high-flown principles of his had landed him in jail with barn-burners and the like. It was too bad, too. He'd never amounted to much — completely wasted that Harvard education of his — but still, there was a lot of good in Henry.

There wasn't anything odd about Henry Thoreau as a boy; he was very much like every other small-town boy of his day. He was born in Concord in 1817 and as soon as he was old enough to be out of his mother's sight he began to explore his town and the fertile fields that lay around it. Concord didn't cover a lot of ground — only 2000 people lived there — but it was a perfect piece of the world for the boy Henry Thoreau. All the conveniences of civilization were there: the church, the post office, the grocer, the barber, the shoemaker and, best of all, just a few minutes' walk away there was the countryside, unspoiled, almost untouched by man.

As Henry grew up he spent every minute that he didn't have to be in school outdoors. He walked out past the town limits, through the cornfields and the wheat fields, climbed over the farmers' stone fences and roamed through the thickly wooded hills beyond. In the leafy gloom of the forest he would glide from tree to tree, being careful not to make a sound, pretending to be one of the Indians who had lived in those very woods not so long before. He kept his eyes peeled for animal tracks and he set traps and, when his father thought he was old enough, he stalked proudly through the woods with a gun. He fished and swam in Concord's lakes and streams all through the hot New England summers and it was said of him that he had an Indian's skill with a canoe. In the winters he skated on the frozen ponds near his home. And he was happy. His father's pencil-making business didn't bring in a lot of money but there was always enough and his family was close-knit, loving and undemanding. The only remarkable thing about Henry Thoreau's boyhood was that he always remembered it as "ecstasy."

At Harvard Thoreau was something of a lone wolf — by necessity and by choice. He wore a green coat to chapel in defiance of the rules that required black; he didn't have a black coat but he must have carried himself as though green was what he wanted to wear because his classmates thought he was purposely being "different." He stayed away from the rollicking student social life around him because it was too expensive for him in both money and time. He didn't have much of the first and he thought he had better ways of spending the second; when the pranks were being played he was in the library reading. He read all the books assigned to him and hundreds more besides. He was looking for something that his academic courses seemed to skirt. The core of life, what living meant, happiness — these were what concerned him most, and the more books he read, the more lectures he heard and the more classes he attended, the more he became convinced that they could be found in the simple, natural, half-wild life he had led as a boy.

Thoreau's thoughts were running in exactly the opposite direction from those of his fellow New Englanders. While he was deciding that simplicity was a key to happiness, most people were busy complicating their lives with the wonderful new inventions of the Industrial Age. Factory towns were springing up wherever a waterfall promised the power to drive machines. Railroad cars were rushing to the cities with raw materials from the countryside and hurrying back with the machine-made clothing and furniture that the country people had suddenly decided they needed. Fortunes were being made in shoe factories, steel foundries and textile mills. While Thoreau was thinking longingly of the slow pace of his boyhood days, New England had fallen in love with speed. People were fascinated with how far and how fast they could travel on the railroads and were awestruck at the wonders of telegraphic communication. Yesterday a Concord merchant had to travel two or three hours in a stagecoach to reach Boston, nineteen miles away; now men were hurtling through the countryside at thirty miles an hour and their words were skimming over telegraph wires at 186,000 miles a second.

By the time Thoreau had completed his four years at Harvard he was definitely out of tune with his times. He had flatly rejected all three of the fields that Harvard graduates were expected to enter. He would not enter the ministry because he was sure that he could find God more easily in nature and in men than in the churches. He shied away from the legal profession because it seemed to him that lawyers and judges were so entangled in the law that they couldn't honestly weigh its justice. And trade? No, trade degraded a man by chaining him to the eternal chore of making money. What would he do then? He would go on looking for what was real in life. But how would he earn his living? That didn't trouble Thoreau; he was sure that once back in Concord he could find a way to make some money, a way that would leave him time for his "proper pursuits."

It was four years later and two old men were sitting in the sunshine on a bench in front of Concord's general store. They were an island of calm and serenity in the sea of bustling activity around them. Horse-drawn carts filled with market produce rumbled over the ruts of Main Street; housewives hurried in and out of the grocer's and the dry-goods store; farmers hitched their teams in front of the post office and went over to the tavern for a glass of rum and the latest word on the market prices; and, as the whistle of the Fitchburg Railroad's locomotive signaled the imminent arrival of the Boston train, children raced down the street to the depot. The two old men sat back peacefully and pulled on their pipes and talked. Specifically, they gossiped:

What was John Thoreau's boy Henry doing these days? Nothing again. And what happened to that school him and his brother were running? It had done pretty good but when young John took so sick it appeared like Henry didn't have any heart to go on with it. Seemed a shame, didn't it, all that time passed and that good education and him still not settled on what he was going to do? Must be something to him though — after all he was thick with that Emerson

fellow and all his literary friends. Yes, there must be some-
thing to Henry but one thing was sure — he hadn't rightly
fitted into anyplace yet.

If Thoreau had heard the two old gossips he would have
said that they were both right and wrong. It was true that
he was at loose ends again as far as a career was concerned
but they were wrong about his not fitting in anyplace. He
fitted into Concord, he thought, like a hand in a glove. In
Concord he had everything he could ever want or need;
first and best there were his beloved woods, fields and
streams; then there were his parents, his sisters, his aunts
and his uncle, all of whom he loved and all of whom took
and cherished him as he was, with or without a career; and,
since he'd come back from Harvard, there was Ralph Waldo
Emerson and the fascinating discussions that were always
going on at his house.

While Thoreau was still at college Ralph Waldo Emerson
had come to Concord to live and to finish his collection of
essays which he called *Nature*. He was by that time well
known as an intellectual "shocker"; he had left the ministry
when his highly individual views on religion clashed with
those of his church, and his speech to the Harvard Divinity
School, in which he maintained that God was in man, was
considered so heretical that thirty years would pass before
he would be invited to speak at Harvard again. But his
ideas on nature impressed Henry Thoreau the most. Modern man, said Emerson, was taking from nature everything
he needed to supply his material wants but, at the same
time, he was losing his greatest heritage, his capacity to see
nature's beauty and to feel her joy. Poring over Emerson's
little book, Thoreau was thrilled — this man's thoughts were
flowing in the same current that his own had taken.

When Thoreau came back to Concord it was only natural

that he was drawn into the whirlwind of discussion, debate and argument that lived in Emerson's parlor. A whole group of noted literary men and women had come to Concord and had gathered around the sage of New England to discuss the burning issues of the day: slavery, democracy, religion, education. Calling themselves Transcendentalists, they rejected all the formal, stale systems of thought that America had inherited from Europe and sought for new, fresh approaches to American life. William Ellery Channing, the poet; Bronson Alcott, the advocate of "progressive" education; Nathaniel Hawthorne, the novelist, and Margaret Fuller, the precocious literary light, all drifted in and out of Emerson's house and all found the gruff young boy, Henry Thoreau, a refreshing, if puzzling, addition to their company.

Thoreau was, by that time, so much of a rebel against the accepted ways of doing things that he appeared odd to even this special group, itself set apart by its purely intellectual interests from the rest of the Concord townspeople. When Thoreau sat in Emerson's parlor his deep-set blue eyes seemed to burn with an extraordinary intensity beneath his heavy brows and Emerson noted admiringly that his first instinct on hearing a positive statement was to contradict it, "so impatient was he of the limitations of our daily thought." Emerson added that he found Thoreau's attitude "a little chilling to the social affections" and when Hawthorne's young wife first met Thoreau she thought he was rude. His appearance didn't help him to make a good first impression; according to Hawthorne he was "ugly as sin, long-nosed and queer-mouthed" and his manners took some getting used to; he used to stride into Emerson's house without warning and often he'd leave just as abruptly. But these were sensitive, discerning people and, though Thoreau never put himself out to be agreeable, they saw beyond his rough exterior to the integrity and basic amiability that were the man himself. After getting to know him, young Mrs. Hawthorne wrote, "Mr. Thoreau has risen above all his arrogance of manner and is as gentle, simple, ruddy and meek as all geniuses should be," and her husband said, "His ugliness is of an honest and agreeable fashion and becomes him better than beauty."

There was something about the young man that made him especially appealing to the Transcendentalists. They all spent a great deal of time thinking and talking and writing about the simple life and the joys to be found in nature but, of them all, only Thoreau knew nature intimately. He seemed to bring the countryside right into their midst; Bronson Alcott said his thoughts were "scented of mountain and field, breezes and rippling springs" and Hawthorne compared conversations with him to "hearing the wind among the boughs of a forest tree."

Thoreau was at his best with children and all his life they were drawn to him as to a magnet. He told them stories, took them berrying and taught them the lore of the woods. He knew all the best places to find arrowheads and other reminders of Concord's Indian past. Even after his beloved brother's illness and subsequent death put an end to Thoreau's schoolteaching career the town children continued to come to him as an authority on all things natural, certain of his knowledge and sure of his regard for them. One Concord boy told of asking Thoreau if the snakes in the millpond could hurt him if he went near them. Thoreau said they couldn't and offered to show him why not. Together they walked to the millpond and,

> . . . there was a big snake fast asleep. Mr. T. quietly stept up and clasped him around the body, a little below the head; whereat Mr. Snake began to wake up

and squirm, and coil himself around the arm of his
captor. He then called my attention to the open mouth
of the reptile, and said, "You see he has no jawbone;
he cannot bite; he sucks in his food; and as for a sting
in his tail that you may have heard the boys talk of —
you can see for yourself there is none," — pinching
the tail. "So you may be assured you will get no harm
if you come in contact with the very king of the water
snakes." And I never had any fear of them after that
day.

After he gave up teaching Thoreau earned his living in a
variety of ways, none of which was considered by the Concord townspeople to be a credit to his education. He had a
natural mathematical aptitude and was much in demand as
a surveyor. He lived at Emerson's house for a while, earning
his keep by doing handyman work, gardening and keeping
of accounts. Later he devoted some time to his family's
pencil-making business and he invented a new type of pen-
cil that was greatly admired. He considered all these occupations, however, to be merely ways of earning the money
he needed for the necessities of life and he felt that his main
business was observing and writing about the basic essence
of life which he found in the woods and meadows around
Concord.

He was outdoors almost every waking moment. A farmer
walking through the early morning mist to where he had
left his plow the night before might see Thoreau perched
on the stone wall that bordered the field and, later in the
day, he might catch a glimpse of him on the crest of a hill,
striding off toward the woods. Even on dark winter days
when the farmer stayed close to his stove, Henry was out.
"I was self-appointed inspector of snow-storms and rain-
storms," he wrote, "and did my duty faithfully; surveyor, if

not of highways, then of forest paths and all across-lot
routes, keeping them open, and ravines bridged and passable
at all seasons . . ." He could prophesy the weather by the
clouds and he took pride in finding his way unerringly
through the woods on moonless nights. At Emerson's sug-
gestion he kept a journal and in it he wrote about the birds
and the small animals that burrowed in the fields and rustled
through the leaves under the tall firs and sumachs. He knew
the habits of the fish in the ponds, and woodchucks, minks
and otters would come closer to him than to other humans.
This was Thoreau's happiness and he worked only to afford
the leisure to pursue it.

The Concord townspeople thought Thoreau was fritter-
ing his life away but he thought the hard-working farmers
and merchants were the time-wasters. Reflecting on his
neighbors "whose misfortune it was to have inherited farms,
houses, barns, cattle and farming tools," he pitied them.
Tied to the never-ending chores of tilling their forty or fifty
acres of land and caring for the animals they needed to work
their fields, they seemed to be the slaves of their possessions.
They were too busy to take a day off and consider the meaning of their lives. One day of a farmer's hard work led in-
exorably into the next.

The merchants who lived in Concord seemed to Thoreau
to be no better off than the farmers. They sat at their desks
from dawn to dusk working to pay for their fine houses. As
Thoreau saw it, these men were exchanging a major portion
of their lives for the dubious advantage of owning a house
which, needing to be furnished and periodically swept,
washed, dusted, repainted and reroofed, then became another link in the chain that bound its owner to a life of toil.
He especially hated to see a man making himself sick with
hard work in order to put aside money against the possi-

bility of his falling ill. "The mass of men," Thoreau concluded, "lead lives of quiet desperation."

He had been studying the works of the ancient Chinese
and Hindu philosophers and, with the exception of Emerson's *Nature*, nothing he'd read had excited him so much.
To find reality, the ancient wisemen had said, a man must
do what he thinks is right, learn to depend on himself for
what he needs, live simply and want little. These were the
very conclusions that Thoreau, himself, had reached.

All at once it came to him that he should act on his convictions. It seemed to him that he had a duty to himself
and to his neighbors to prove that if a man simplified his
life he could feed and shelter himself and still have plenty
of time for the serious business of living. There was a spot
out in the woods near Walden Pond that he had had his eye
on. He would go out there, he decided, and conduct an
experiment in living.

2

Two Years in the Woods

IN THE SPRING of 1845 Thoreau borrowed Bronson Alcott's ax and, in the woods on the edge of Walden Pond, about a mile from the outskirts of Concord, he started to build himself a house. Alone in the quiet splendor of the tall trees, he cut down young white pines for timber, dug a cellar in the side of a hill and made a chimney from stones he'd carried up from the pond in his arms. It wasn't much of a house when he'd finished but it was just what he wanted. It measured 19 feet by 15 feet, had a door at one end and a fireplace at the other, an attic, a closet and a large window at each side. Proud of his handiwork, he wrote in his journal, "I intend to build me a house which will surpass any on the main street in Concord in grandeur and luxury, as soon as it pleases me as much and will cost me no more than my present one."

Next, he planted two and a half acres of beans, potatoes, corn, peas and turnips. He had to buy a few of the building materials for his house and he had to hire a man and a team of horses to break the ground for his vegetable gardens but he earned most of the money he laid out by doing stretches of surveying, carpentry and day labor. Eight months after he started living in the woods he listed his total expenses for his house, his food, clothing and fuel and found that they amounted to only $25.21¾. That, he figured, was coming very close to the self-reliance he aimed at.

By building his own house and raising his own food Thoreau felt that he'd made contact with the very stuff of which life is made. His house, though adequate for his needs, was neither so grand nor so costly that he felt anchored to it; if it should burn or if his crops should fail he would lose practically nothing in terms of money and time spent. Happily he concluded that living in this way he would only have to work at manual labor for six weeks of the year and could spend the other forty-six in unhurried pursuit of his happiness. At Walden Pond Henry Thoreau had shelter, food, good health and, best of all, his cherished leisure.

They were there again, the two old friends, on the bench in front of the general store. Puffing out clouds of tobacco smoke, they watched the Concord townspeople hurrying about their errands and, enjoying the pale warmth of the winter sun, they talked. There was a lot they could talk about: it was early in the year 1845 and the country was in a turmoil over the slavery issue; there was talk of secession in the South; the fate of the vast Texas territory hung in the balance — but they were old men and their world had shrunk until it held only what they could see and the people they knew. They talked about Concord and its citizens and, especially, about the town's "character," Henry Thoreau:

Was Henry still out there to Walden Pond? He was, and it appeared like he was going to stay there for quite a bit. Must be mighty lonesome out there so far from other folks. Henry said not. His Aunt Maria'd been out there to see him and she'd found him right happy and snug. Sometimes his fancy friends came too and when they did he set out the three chairs he'd got in the pine needles in front of his cabin and acted like the woods was his parlor. Wasn't it a funny thing Henry never married? He was thinking of it once. Folks said him and his brother John loved the same girl but she wouldn't have either of them. Her pa didn't like the

Thoreaus' kind of radical ways. After that it seemed like Henry decided he wasn't the marrying kind . . . Not the sociable kind either. Never would join anything. Even signed off from the church. Wasn't it a queer way Henry'd picked to do? Whatever in the world could he find to do with himself out there in the woods?

Thoreau lived at Walden Pond for two years and in his own way he was busy all the time. Part of each day he devoted to providing himself with the necessities of life: he drew drinking water from the pond, he fished for his supper, he baked his own bread and roasted tender young ears of corn in the ashes of a wood fire and he hoed his beans, but most of the time he did what most men would call nothing and what he believed was living life to its fullest. Sitting on his doorstep, or walking through the woods, or stretching out at full length and gazing into the clear depths of the pond, Thoreau watched and listened to the teeming natural life around him and tried to relate what he saw and heard to the lives of men. As they came to him he wrote his thoughts in the notebook he carried with him and later, molded and polished, they were transcribed into his journal. From his journal he culled the collection of essays, *Walden,* which he published in 1854.

Was it, as many of the Concord townspeople thought, despair and indifference to his neighbors that sent Thoreau to live alone in the woods? Far from it. In the pages of *Walden* the reader sees Thoreau as he really was — content, joyous and so concerned with his fellow men that he wanted, above all, to communicate the wonderful answers to life's questions that he had found.

"I went to the woods," Thoreau wrote, "because I wished to live deliberately, to front only the essential facts of life, and see if I could not learn what it had to teach, and not, when I came to die, discover that I had not lived . . . I wanted to live deep and suck out all the marrow of life . . ."

The marrow of life for Thoreau was a sunny morning when he sat in the doorway of his house from sunrise till noon,

> . . . rapt in a revery, amidst the pines and hickories and sumachs in undisturbed solitude and stillness, while the birds sang around or flitted noiseless through the house . . .

or, as he walked in his shirtsleeves by the stony edge of the pond,

> . . . a delicious evening when the whole body is one sense and imbibes delight through every pore. I go and come with a strange liberty in Nature, as part of herself . . . The bullfrogs trump to usher in the night and the note of the whip-poor-will is borne on the rippling wind from over the water. Sympathy with the fluttering alder and poplar leaves almost takes my breath away.

or, winter afternoons when

> . . . I frequently tramped eight or ten miles through the deepest snow to keep an appointment with a beech tree, or a yellow birch, or an old acquaintance among the pines.

There in the woods Thoreau found the truths he'd been seeking, there was the proof that life need not be made up only of hurry, worry and sweat. In the *Walden* essays he compared his life to that of his neighbors, hoping that if only men could see the folly of their ways they would lift their eyes from the furrows they plowed and the rows of tiny figures they entered in their ledger-books.

Walden brought Thoreau a small measure of fame during his later life and, after his death, it established him as one of America's foremost writers and philosophers. Henry Thoreau, Concord's "time-waster," stands revealed in the pages of his essays as a man who, having studied the small portion of the earth he inhabits, is world-wise. Discussing such homely topics as "The Bean-Field," "Sounds," "The Pond in Winter," he is economist, naturalist, critic, optimist, philosopher and poet. Under his pen the sights and sounds that he knew came alive, carrying with them an insight into the meaning of men's lives. Concise, witty, direct and vigorous, Thoreau's prose style mirrors the man and brings his Concord, his beloved piece of the world, vibrant and fresh, down across the years.

Walden secured Thoreau's place in history as one of the first truly American philosophers and as an outstanding man of letters but he was to know still another fame. "Civil Disobedience," an essay he published in 1849, showed him to be a pioneer political reformer. How did Henry Thoreau, deliberately turning away from what he called "this restless, nervous, bustling, trivial 19th century," get involved in politics? The answer lies in his sense of duty. He had always felt his responsibilities keenly: to himself, to live his life fully, and to his fellow men to point out the meaningless and futile character of their lives. Events were to force him to admit still another obligation, that of a citizen to an imperfect state. In the summer of 1846 he declared that a man's primary duty to his state, when its interests are in conflict with his conscience, is to resist it.

3

A Night in Jail

IN JULY, 1846, Henry Thoreau refused to pay his tax to the State of Massachusetts. "Another example of Henry's eccentricity," said the Concord townspeople. "I quietly declare war with the State, after my fashion," said Thoreau.

The state only expected to exact $1.50 from him, a small sum he could easily have earned in a day or two of gardening or surveying work, so it wasn't a question of his not being able to raise the money. It was a question of conscience. When his neighbor, the tax collector, came around to see him Thoreau explained that he was in rebellion against the state and his conscience would not allow him to pay tribute to it in the form of taxes.

The tax collector did his duty — unwillingly, we can guess; it is not easy to send a neighbor to jail. One day soon after, when Thoreau walked into town to get a shoe he'd left to be mended at the cobbler's on Court Street, he was arrested and escorted to the Concord jail. He was put in a clean, whitewashed cell and he said he was happy to be there; he felt that in jail a good citizen could best serve an "unjust state."

Thoreau had quarreled with the State of Massachusetts on two counts: first, its support of the American war with Mexico, and second, its support of slavery in the South. The young nation, flushed with success and certain of its "manifest destiny" to expand its influence and landholdings, was engaged in a war with Mexico over the Texas territory. Thoreau was one of many Americans who believed that Mexico had as much right to the disputed land as did the United States and since his time most historians have supported that opinion and have spoken of the Mexican War as a blot on America's record. There had been talk of a United States purchase of the Texas land from Mexico but, when the Mexican government was not immediately receptive to the idea, President Polk sent troops to occupy the Texas territory. In the battles that followed, American armed forces invaded and overran Mexico; American and Mexican lives were lost in a war that Thoreau called "unnecessary and unjust."

At the same time, Thoreau felt that the State of Massachusetts, though it had outlawed slavery in its territory in 1780, was, together with the other northern "free" states, partially to blame for the evils of slavery in the South. He said that while men, women and children were being bought and sold like cattle anyplace in the country and while the United States government was catching runaway slaves and imprisoning them or returning them to their masters, every American must feel responsible. Citizens of the "free" Northern states, he maintained, must either take action against slavery in the South or, by their lack of action, pay homage to the evil they opposed. He decided that he could no longer give his allegiance to the State of Massachusetts while it, in turn, gave its allegiance to a Union containing "slave" states.

Thus, at odds with a government pursuing what he considered to be an unjust war and encouraging the slavery he abhorred, Thoreau refused to pay his tax and went to jail. Struck by the irony of the situation he said, "I could not but smile to see how industriously they locked the door on my meditations, which followed them out again without let or hindrance, and *they* were really all that was dangerous." He had a long conversation with his cellmate, a man who was in jail for barn-burning, and as he lay in his cot that night, listening to the sounds of village life around the jail, Thoreau felt more free than those on the outside who were slaves to an unjust state.

The next morning one of the old men was waiting impatiently when his friend hobbled up to their meeting place. They could just walk down the street a piece to the jail, he suggested — maybe they could see Henry Thoreau looking out through the bars. But his friend brought disappointing news. It wouldn't be any use going down there — Henry had already gone.

But he'd just been arrested the day before. That was so but after dark some veiled female had come down to the jail and paid his tax and the jailer had let him out early in the morning. Whoever it was paid didn't want herself known. It seemed Henry had been right proud to go to jail and would be sure to be hopping mad at whoever pulled himself out so soon. It was most likely his Aunt Maria. His mother wouldn't ever do what Henry didn't want but Maria wouldn't be able to stand seeing him a laughingstock. What had Henry done when the jailer let him out? He'd gone on down to get his shoe at the cobbler's like he'd started out to do when they arrested him. Then he was off to the hills — said something about promising some folks to lead them on a huckleberrying party. Well, it would appear like Henry'd better leave well enough alone after coming off so easy. Maybe so, but Henry was an odd fellow. There was no telling what he'd do now.

Not many people outside of Concord heard about Thoreau's imprisonment and the Concord townspeople unanimously thought his refusal to pay his tax was the gesture of a fool. His had been a small rebellion, short-lived and without observable effect. The hundreds of Americans, also opposed to slavery and the war, whom Thoreau had hoped would follow him to jail, stayed home. Another man might

Henry Thoreau's birthplace in Concord, Massachusetts

Young Thoreau (second from left) and Emerson (wearing top hat) pass the time of day with their fellow townsmen.

Painting by N. C. Wyeth

The Rowse portrait
of Thoreau
as a young man

Houghton Mifflin

Drawing by J. W. Barber of
the central part
of Concord in the early nineteenth century

Culver Pictures Inc.

well have considered the incident closed but Thoreau said in
his journal:

> I feel that, to some extent, the State has fatally in-
> terfered with my just and proper business. It has not
> merely interrupted me in my passage through Court
> Street on errands of trade, but it has, to some extent,
> interrupted me and every man on his onward and up-
> ward path . . . I have found that hollow which I relied
> on for solid.

He felt that he had to pursue his revolution further and
three years later he published "Civil Disobedience," an account of an individual's refusal to cooperate with an evil
system.

In this essay Thoreau brings the citizen face to face with
his conscience and with his government and asks to which
he owes the greater allegiance. Thoreau's own answer is:
"The only obligation which I have a right to assume is to do
at any time what I think right."

Thoreau realized that there are injustices in the best of
governments and, in the interest of serenity, he was willing
to put up with those which worked hardship on himself. He
drew the line at those demands of the state which required
him to help it in its injustice to others. Pointing to the war
and slavery as evils which his tax money helped to support,
he wrote:

> . . . when a sixth of the population of a nation which
> has undertaken to be the refuge of liberty are slaves,
> and a whole country is unjustly overrun and con-
> quered by a foreign army, and subjected to military
> law, I think that it is not too soon for honest men to
> rebel and revolutionize. What makes this duty the

more urgent is the fact that the country so overrun is
not our own, but ours is the invading army.

Thoreau was incensed at those of his countrymen who also
saw the war and slavery as evils and yet, "esteeming themselves children of Washington and Franklin, sit down with
their hands in their pockets, and say that they know not
what to do, and do nothing." He painted a chilling picture
of the results of an unquestioning obedience to an imperfect
state:

> A common and natural result of an undue respect for
> law is, that you may see a file of soldiers, colonel, cap-
> tain, corporal, privates, powder-monkeys, and all,
> marching in admirable order over hill and dale to the
> wars, against their wills, ay, against their common
> sense and consciences, which makes it very steep
> marching indeed, and produces a palpitation of the
> heart. They have no doubt that it is a damnable busi-
> ness in which they are concerned; they are all peace-
> ably inclined. . . .

When Thoreau warned in "Civil Disobedience" of the
danger presented by a tyranny of the majority, many of his
contemporary readers must have thought he had taken leave
of his senses. Americans considered their infant republic to
be a beacon of justice for the world and its Constitution a
bulwark against inequity. Thoreau, however, considered
the will of the majority to be a more polite way of saying
"might makes right" and he was impatient with the Constitution's provisions for dissent. If an American citizen is dis-
satisfied with the way his government is conducting its affairs he can cast his vote against those measures he opposes
or he can circulate petitions denouncing the government's
actions. But, said Thoreau, petitions take too much time and

the vote is too feeble a weapon of protest. If a man is out-voted is he to abandon his convictions and bow to the will of the greater number? Thoreau believed that, on the contrary, a true patriot will resist a tyrannical majority.

These were very outlandish ideas in the eyes of most Americans. A man who rebelled against his government committed treason, they believed, and should be put in jail. Thoreau agreed that he should pay the penalty for his action but insisted that his refusal to pay his tax was the act of a good citizen serving his government with his conscience. If other Americans also refused to pay, Thoreau was sure that together they could conduct an effective protest even though they were a physically powerless minority. Comparing the government to a system of machinery, Thoreau showed how a small minority, by refusing to pay their taxes and going to jail, could clog the gears of that machinery. This would be, he said, a "peaceable revolution." In jail this dissenting minority would afflict the conscience of the state and, by suffering injustice themselves, would be more eloquent in opposing injustice to others.

Thoreau believed that the whole question came down to this: "Unjust laws exist: shall we be content to obey them, or shall we endeavor to amend them, and obey them until we have succeeded, or shall we transgress them at once? His own answer was "Break the law."

Thoreau's grievances against his government concerned the Mexican War and slavery. The Mexican War is now little more than a few paragraphs in the history books and slavery was abolished a hundred years ago. Yet "Civil Disobedience" lives today as it always will live while there are governments and men who question them. Circumstances change but the question remains: Is it my duty as a citizen to obey my government because it is my government or do I, as a patriotic citizen, have a higher duty to resist it when it contradicts my conscience?

Henry Thoreau died in 1862 when he was forty-five years old. His health had been poor for several years but his joy in living never failed. As he lay dying someone asked him if he had made his peace with God and he is reported to have answered, "I was not aware that we had quarrelled."

The ideas set forth in "Civil Disobedience" spread abroad from their birthplace to the farthest corners of the earth. Stirring men's courage and prodding them out of their lethargy, Thoreau's conception of nonviolent resistance to evil has transcended the limits of time and space. Thoreau said of his peaceable revolution, "It matters not how small the beginning may seem to be; what is once well done is done forever." His prophecy was fulfilled; in other times and other places hundreds and then thousands more followed him to jail in peaceful protest against unjust laws.

A little more than fifty years after Thoreau's death, a little brown-skinned man in a South African jail read "Civil Disobedience" and was deeply impressed. Already a peaceable rebel against a repressive government, Mohandas Gandhi, an Indian, found new inspiration in the words of the rebel of Concord, Massachusetts.

II

Mohandas Gandhi

1

Meat and Marriage

Behold the mighty Englishman
He rules the Indian small,
Because being a meat-eater
He is five cubits tall.

IT WAS ONLY a schoolboy jingle but Mohandas Gandhi couldn't get it out of his head. He was fifteen years old and he had never eaten meat; until now he had never even considered the possibility of tasting it. His family were Hindus of the Vaishnava sect and the Vaishnavas adhered to the religious principle of *ahimsa,* or "harmlessness," so strictly that killing animals for food was out of the question for them. But now Mohandas was pulled in two directions. One of his friends, Mehta, had been boasting about how "emancipated" he was; Mehta ate meat and he hinted broadly that a lot of other Indians in Rajkot secretly did the same. It was obvious, Mehta said, that flesh in one's diet made one strong and fearless. "Look at the British," he told Mohandas, "look at me — then look at yourself."

It was quite true that most Englishmen were a lot bigger and seemed much sturdier than most Indians; reflecting on his own skinny arms and legs Mohandas had to admit that they didn't compare at all well with the firmly muscled physique that made Mehta a star in the running and jumping games in which he, himself, made such a miserable showing. And then there were his shameful fears to be taken into account. He was afraid of a hundred things — at night, snakes, burglars and ghosts all lurked in the corners of

his room and he couldn't get to sleep unless there was a light
burning nearby. He was a coward — he admitted it. Could
it be that eating meat would change all that? Mehta had
assured him that when enough Indians became "emancipated" the British would be forced out of India. Was it possible that a nation of meat-eating Indians could become
powerful enough to free their country from foreign rule?
Finally, Mohandas succumbed to Mehta's arguments. He
would try eating meat.

Secrecy was of the utmost importance so Mehta took
Mohandas to a lonely spot by the river and there, over a
wood fire, he cooked a piece of goat meat. When Mohandas
ate it he felt sick. Mehta told him that that was only because
the taste was so new to him — he knew where they could
rent a kitchen for an afternoon and the next time he would
prepare the meat more tastefully and Mohandas would like
it better. Mehta was right — after several more attempts
Mohandas found that he was actually enjoying the forbidden
food. But, just when he was beginning to look forward to
the secret feasts, he decided that he would have to call a halt
to the whole business. Buying the meat and renting the
kitchen had become much too expensive and besides his
lack of appetite at home was beginning to be noticed. Once,
when his father asked him why he was not eating more he
had answered that he had a pain in his stomach which, since
he was forcing himself to eat a second supper, was quite
true, but he knew that if he was questioned more closely he
would have to either confess or lie and he could do neither.
He couldn't face his parents' horror at finding out that he
had eaten meat and since they had always laid so much
stress on the necessity for telling the truth he couldn't possibly lie to them. He would have to put off that particular

kind of self-strengthening while his parents were alive. If
he were to play a part in freeing India he would have to rely
on something other than physical strength.

The time was 1884. India had been a colony of the British
Empire for twenty-six years but Englishmen had ruled India
for a long time before that.

Early in the seventeenth century they had come with the
British East India Company as traders, in search of India's
fabled wealth of gold, spices and exotic fabrics. Establishing
trading posts on the Indian coast, the English took advantage
of disputes between provincial Indian warlords to increase
their landholdings and their influence. Other European
countries, especially France and the Netherlands, competed
with Britain for control of India's riches and there was open
warfare between rival trading companies but, finally, British
influence reigned supreme. In 1818 the British East India
Company governed all of India.

By that time England had become a manufacturing nation and, protecting her own infant textile industries, she
slapped high tariffs on the Indian calicoes and gossamer
sheer linens that the English people had been buying in
huge quantities. The harshly taxed Indian fabrics became
too expensive — nobody in England wanted them any more.
As India's once flourishing export trade with Britain dried
up, millions of Indians were thrown out of work; trees grew
up in the streets of India's industrial cities. As Britain took
India's raw cotton to feed her own industrial looms, as the
Indian people saw their gold and spices flowing across the
sea to England while they grew poorer and poorer, resentment spread through the land. In 1857 a bloody uprising,
the Sepoy Mutiny, broke out, but it was quickly crushed.
The next year Queen Victoria announced to the world

that India was a colony of the British Empire and since
that time most Indians had come to accept the fact that
their white masters were there to stay.

But, in 1869, an Indian child, Mohandas Gandhi, was born
and this child, grown to a man, would hold in his hands the
fate of the "mighty Englishman" in India.

The Gandhi family lived in the northwest Indian state of
Rajkot, and Karamchand — or Kaba, as he was called —
Gandhi earned his living as the financial adviser to the native
prince. Unlike the great cities of India, the Rajkot section of
the country was still relatively untouched by Western in-
fluences and the Gandhis lived by the same customs and traditions as had their ancestors for generations before them.

Young Mohandas's life centered around his mother. He
was a homely, big-eared boy, skinny, rather frail and very
shy. He used to run home the minute school was over for
the day, afraid that his schoolmates would tease him if he lin-
gered and anxious to be with his mother, who made him feel
secure and happy. Though Putlibai Gandhi was a loving
and gentle mother, the example she set for her children was
one of austerity and strict self-discipline. Her religion domi-
nated her life. During the four months of the rainy season
each year when Hindus are required to undertake limited
fasts she would set herself additional religious tasks and
Mohandas always remembered one particular rainy season
when his mother vowed not to touch food on the days when
she did not see the sun. Mohandas, his two brothers and his
sister would eagerly scan the overcast skies, running to tell
their mother whenever the sun broke through for a minute.
She would rush outdoors with them and if, by that time, the
sun had disappeared behind a cloud, she would tell her
children cheerfully that it didn't matter, that God just didn't
want her to eat that day.

The discovery of truth, Putlibai Gandhi told her children, is a Hindu's most important goal in life and young Mohandas, in his quest for truth, took pride in being honest at all times. Once, when the District Inspector paid a visit to his school, his teacher, noticing that the boy had misspelled the word "kettle" and wanting the Inspector to see a perfect spelling record for the class, tried to persuade Mohandas to copy the correct spelling from the boy next to him. Mohandas would not be persuaded and his was the only blemish on the class record.

The Hindu doctrine of ahimsa became a living reality for Mohandas one day when he was sitting with his mother and suddenly saw a deadly scorpion scuttling across the floor toward his mother's bare foot. He cried out in fright but she calmly allowed the scorpion to crawl up on her heel and then she gently picked up the insect with her shawl and, taking it to an open window, she shook it free. "Now," she told her son, "it will neither harm me nor I it." Truth, harmlessness, self-discipline. All these were prescribed by the Hindu religion and Mohandas saw his mother practice them faithfully in her daily life.

All at once, when Mohandas was thirteen, there was a great stirring in the Gandhi household and the boy sensed that the excitement had something to do with him. When he was told that he was about to be married he didn't think it at all strange. For a long time he had suspected that he was betrothed; Hindu parents usually arranged betrothals for their children when they were six or seven though the children were rarely informed of the arrangements. Now, at thirteen, Mohandas knew that it was time he was married and, trusting his parents' judgment, he was sure that a suitable bride had been found for him. All the women in his house — his mother, his sister, and his sisters-in-law — were busy with preparations for his wedding and Mohandas, the proud center of everybody's attention, thoroughly enjoyed the hubbub. He rather looked forward to having "a strange girl to play with" and, knowing that it was a Hindu wife's duty to be unquestioningly obedient to her husband's every wish, he couldn't wait to play the role of "lord and master."

Kasturbai, Mohandas's bride, was also thirteen. She was a beautiful young girl, the lovingly spoiled daughter of the well-to-do Nakanji family. She came to marriage well equipped with a trousseau of lovely saris and jewels and a rudimentary knowledge of the household arts but, as Mohandas soon discovered, she had a spunky, independent nature with wishes of her own that often clashed with his. Establishing himself as Kasturbai's lord and master was no easy matter. Immature and unsure of himself, he tried to enforce her obedience by imposing all sorts of restrictions on her activities and, liking the picture of himself as a jealous husband, he forbade her to go anywhere without his permission. Kasturbai thought it was ridiculous that she should not be able to go to the temple or to visit her friends whenever she wanted to and she went out of her way to disobey her boy-husband. Bitter quarrels were the result. Whole days passed when the married children refused to speak to each other.

But each quarrel was made up before another began and Mohandas found himself becoming very fond of his lovely wife in spite of her unseemly independence. As was customary for Hindu girls, Kasturbai's education had been concerned solely with the skills she would need as a wife and a mother; she felt no need of more learning, but the fact that she was illiterate bothered Mohandas and he made elaborate plans to teach her all he was learning in school. But, since Hindu custom did not allow young husbands and wives to

meet during the daylight hours, Mohandas made little head-
way on his teaching project. Kasturbai was a reluctant pupil
and all too often Mohandas the teacher allowed Mohandas
the ardent husband to push him aside.

Marriage didn't change Mohandas's daily routine. Kasturbai lived in his father's house but she stayed in seclusion
with the women of the household all day and after school
Mohandas was free to do as he chose. He had overcome
some of his shyness and now, as he began to spend his leisure
time with his school friends, the necessity for telling the
truth became a real problem to him. His uncle threw away
cigarette butts and, when no one was around, Mohandas and
his friends picked them up and smoked them. This was certainly wrong and if his parents asked him about it he would
have to tell the truth. But he was careful never to be seen
smoking and so the truth was precariously preserved. He
applied the same kind of compromise with the truth to his
meat-eating experiments but when he got himself into a
much more complicated moral position he was overwhelmed
with guilt. His older brother, Karsandas, was in debt.
Mohandas knew about it and, thinking to help his brother,
he stole a piece of gold from Karsandas's bracelet, sold the
gold, and paid off the debt. But then his conscience began
to bother him badly. His guilt lay on him so heavily that he
knew only a full confession to his father could ease his torment. Afraid, not of the punishment he would receive, but
of the anguish he would cause his father, he confessed in a
note which he silently handed to him. It was a painful moment for both father and son. Reading the note, Karamchand
Gandhi wept and the boy knew when he saw his father's
tears that he had been forgiven.

Karamchand was already very ill at the time and he died
not long afterward. Mohandas had nursed him and cared

for him lovingly, massaging his legs daily in an effort to relieve his pain, but on one particular night he allowed his uncle to take over the massaging and he hurried to Kasturbai. That was the night that Karamchand Gandhi died and Mohandas never forgave himself for allowing his desire for his young wife to draw him from his dying father's side.

When Mohandas finished high school a trusted friend advised the Gandhi family to send the boy to England for legal training. He thought that in England Mohandas could most easily and cheaply get the higher education that would enable him to contribute to the support of his family. The prestige attached to an English professional education would, everyone believed, assure him of a well-paying post on his return to India. At first Putlibai Gandhi wouldn't hear of it; she was afraid that Mohandas would be corrupted by so much exposure to Western influence. But when her son vowed that he would touch neither meat nor wine while he was away she agreed to let him go.

Mohandas was overjoyed at the idea of going to England. He was yearning for some adventure before settling down completely to the life of a responsible married man. And, too, he was anxious to find out what the "mighty Englishman" was like in his homeland.

He would miss Kasturbai but he was sure that the separation would be good for both of them. They still quarreled a great deal and perhaps, when they were both older, there would be less tension between them. Kasturbai would get along very well without him; his family would take good care of her and she would go on frequent visits to her own parents. Besides, she had been paying very little attention to him since the birth of their baby. A boy, Harilal, had been born a few months earlier and though the eighteen-year-old Mohandas was proud of being a father, he found the baby very dull. Harilal would be four years old when his father returned to India and Mohandas hoped he would be more interesting then.

Parting from his mother was the hardest for Mohandas. He had been married for five years but his mother was still the woman he loved the most.

2

In England

ON THE BOAT going to England, the subject of meat loomed large again. The food served at the shipboard meals was all unfamiliar to Mohandas and, taking no chances on breaking his vow to his mother, he lived mainly on a stock of fruits and cakes he had brought with him from home. An English passenger, taking a kindly interest in the Indian boy, told him that once they reached the Bay of Biscay he had best forget his prejudices against meat and begin eating it or he would not be able to survive in the cold English climate. Everywhere Mohandas turned he got the same advice. Everyone wanted to be friendly, everyone wanted to be helpful, everyone wanted him to eat meat.

Arriving in London he struck out bravely in the bewildering welter of strange new people and customs. He found lodgings, enrolled for his course of studies and made friends. But the difficulties of sticking to a vegetarian diet in a meat-eating society threatened to overwhelm him. Though he tried to be unobtrusive about it Mohandas knew that his fellow lodgers noticed when he skipped the meat portion of the meal and when he insisted on knowing what went into the soup it was obvious that everybody thought he was ridiculous. Worse, he was always hungry. Eggs, being an animal product, were also forbidden to him by his vow, the bland way the English cooked their vegetables didn't tempt him at all and though he tried he couldn't seem to fill up on oatmeal, breads and desserts. During his first days in England hunger sharpened his natural feelings of homesickness and he used to lie in his bed at night and weep; he was haunted by memories not of his wife and child, but of his mother and the delights of Indian food. Finally, he discovered a vegetarian restaurant in London and, his stomach filled for the first time since he had come to England, he began to feel better.

As he got to know some of the people who habitually ate at the restaurant, Mohandas discussed the subject of diets with them. Vegetarianism was a new health-fad in England at the time and its disciples were convinced that they had found the one and only road to robust health. Mohandas had been abstaining from meat only to keep his vow to his mother but now, influenced by the enthusiasm of his new friends, he became a vegetarian by choice. A meatless diet, he decided, was not only the healthiest but also — an important consideration to a young man with limited funds — the most economical.

No sooner did he start his law studies than Mohandas began to model himself after the debonair English students whom he admired. He was very self-conscious about the clumsy impression his vegetarianism made on his fellow students and he decided to make himself acceptable in polite English society in every other respect. He bought himself a high silk hat and a fashionably cut suit and learned the art of tying a cravat. He should learn to dance, he thought, and to play the violin. Before long his goal of becoming "an English gentleman" had obscured everything else. He signed up for dancing lessons, found a violin teacher and invested in a violin. But within a few months, discouragement and a depleted pocketbook brought him back to his senses. His dancing teacher despaired of ever teaching him a sense of rhythm and he was getting nowhere with the violin. It wasn't fair, Mohandas decided, to use his family's money on such "frills." Besides, his law studies were suffering. Suddenly he realized that there were no real short cuts to becoming a gentleman. If his character made him one, so much the better, but it was clear that for the present he had best forget about all the "polishing" lessons and concentrate on the study of the law that had brought him to England.

Mohandas liked the English people he met. At home in India the only Englishmen he knew had seemed aloof and conceited. They kept to themselves for the most part and when they occasionally met socially with Indians they acted condescending, as though they were doling out favors. Here in England, however, the people were warm and human and Mohandas had no trouble making friends. He was a homely, insignificant-looking young man but his personality seemed to reach out and take hold of people. One English matron found him so engaging that she invited him to her home often and she left him alone with a young woman friend of hers so often that Mohandas began to feel acutely uncomfortable. Taking his cue from the other Indian students in London, he hadn't mentioned the fact that he was a married man; now it seemed that he must. He confessed in a letter to the English lady and waited anxiously for her reply. There was a real possibility that she would be angry at his deceiving her. But she was not angry — she was amused. He must come the next Sunday as planned, she wrote; she and her young friend were looking forward to hearing all about his child marriage and to laughing at how worried he had been.

It was during his stay in England that Mohandas became seriously interested in the subject of religion for the first time. The Hindu precepts of truth and ahimsa had been a part of his daily life at home but he had never had any formal training in Hinduism; when he had gone to the Vaishnava temple with his parents he had been moved more by a sense of duty than by religious interest. Now he began to read the Bhagavad-Gita, the sacred book of Hinduism, and he was deeply impressed.

The Gita is a long, beautiful poem instructing the reader that he can become one with Brahman, or God, by the practice of a rigorous self-discipline and an undeviating pursuit of the truth. Man must become "desireless," says the Gita, and he must school himself to do what he believes is right without even considering the consequences of his actions. He must cast off hatred, for hate and desire are the veils of illusion concealing truth and reality. Mohandas was struck by the wisdom he found in the ancient poem and from that time forward it was always to the Gita that he turned for inspiration.

During the same period Gandhi also read the Bible. The Old Testament meant little to him but the New Testament, and especially the Sermon on the Mount, seemed to go straight to his heart. The verses: "But I say unto you, That ye resist not evil: but whosoever shall smite thee on thy right cheek, turn to him the other also. And if any man take away thy coat, let him have thy cloak also" delighted him — they were completely in tune with the teachings of the Gita. These words of Jesus showed him that a belief in "harmlessness" was also a basic part of the Christian religion. Must they then be such strangers to each other, Hindus and Christians, East and West? When he had first arrived in England Gandhi had been blinded by the external matters of dress and custom that set men apart from each other. Now, studying religion, he began to see the ties that bind all men of conscience together.

English law examinations were not difficult in Gandhi's day. Most of the English students didn't even bother to read all the assigned texts and they assured the young Indian that

he needn't either. The examiners were notoriously "gener-
ous," they told him; he'd be sure to "get by" — he should
spend more time enjoying himself. But Gandhi wanted to
do more than get by. He struggled through every one of his
dry lawbooks and he passed the examinations easily. Nevertheless, he began to worry about his future; he knew that
there was a vast difference between having studied the law
and being competent to practice it, and he was apprehensive
about his ability to earn a living in his homeland. He had
learned nothing of Indian law and he was ignorant of Indian
techniques in the law courts. He was slightly encouraged
when a prominent English lawyer who had befriended him
assured him that unfailing industry and honesty would
eventually turn him into an able attorney and, alternating
between hope and despair, he sailed for home.

A sad shock awaited him in Bombay where his elder
brother, Laxmidas, had come to meet him. Longing to see
his mother, Mohandas learned that she had died while he
was in England. The family, wanting to spare him a crush-
ing blow while he was so far from home, had decided not
to tell him of her death until he reached India. His grief was
almost overwhelming and it was only with great effort that
he pulled himself together in preparation for taking up life
anew, as a lawyer, as a husband and as a father of a four-
year-old son.

Life at home was discouraging in every respect. Gandhi's
unreasonable jealousy of Kasturbai, which he had hoped
would be vanquished by the long separation, returned in
full force. His renewed efforts to teach her reading and
writing came to nothing and there was little peace between
husband and wife. Unable to find clients in his home province of Rajkot who were willing to trust themselves to an
untried boy, Mohandas returned to Bombay to study Indian
law and to get experience in the High Court.

In Bombay Gandhi's conscience barred his path to success. It was the common practice of young lawyers competing for cases to pay a commission to whoever brought them their clients. Gandhi believed the custom was unethical and refused to go along with it; as a result his practice was almost nonexistent. He managed to get one case without paying a commission but once in court his nerve deserted him and he found himself speechless. He had to pay another lawyer to defend his client and he hurried from the court determined to stay away until he found more courage.

Disheartened after six fruitless months in Bombay and wanting to cut down expenses, Mohandas returned to Rajkot and there kept moderately busy doing legal detail work which his brother sent his way. Even this work meant compromises with his conscience and he was so exasperated that when, in 1893, the Indian firm of Dada Abdulla and Company offered him a job as legal adviser to their people in South Africa, he grasped at the opportunity. He would only be paid a small salary, plus a round-trip first-class passage and his living expenses while in South Africa, but he didn't care. It was a way of breaking out of the frustrating rut he was in and he'd be certain to gain useful experience. Besides, the job was to last only a year.

Again Kasturbai would be left behind, this time with two children — Harilal, aged five, and a baby boy, Manilal, born in 1892. Mohandas didn't like the idea of leaving Kasturbai and their sons but he wasn't worried about them. They would stay with Laxmidas and his family and he would contribute his salary to help with expenses. Kasturbai wept as he prepared to leave and Gandhi tried to comfort her: "We will be together again within a year," he promised.

3

The Color Bar

A LAWYER must travel first-class; there was no doubt in
Gandhi's mind about that but when he reached the port of
Bombay he was told that all the first-class passages on the
ship for South Africa had already been booked. What was
he to do? He was a lawyer, an unsuccessful one it was true,
but a lawyer nonetheless and he couldn't possibly sail as a
deck passenger. He went on board the ship and presented
his problem to the captain. The captain looked Gandhi over
from head to toe. He saw that the young Indian, though
hardly more than a boy, was carefully dressed in a frock
coat and trousers with an impressive turban almost over-
shadowing the slight frame below; he saw serious dark eyes
pleading that the vital matter of self-respect was at stake.
The captain smiled. It was quite true, he said, that all the
regular first-class berths were taken but Mr. Gandhi could,
if he wished, share his own cabin — he would be happy to
have Mr. Gandhi's company. And so it was arranged. His
dignity intact, Mohandas Gandhi left his homeland and set
sail for South Africa, a land that he would find had little
respect for his or any other Indian's dignity.

Abdulla Sheth, a partner in the firm of Dada Abdulla and
Company, met Gandhi at the port of Durban in the province
of Natal. Gandhi noticed immediately that the white men
who knew Abdulla treated him in an offhand manner in
spite of the fact that he was a prominent businessman. Abdulla seemed unconcerned but Gandhi was stung by the
realization that it was Abdulla's brown skin that marked him
for contempt. Abdulla took Gandhi under his wing, intro-

duced him to the legal world of Durban and acquainted him with the facts of life regarding white and nonwhite people in the British colony of South Africa.

All South Africans were classified as either Europeans (white), Negro (native African), Colored (mixed white and Negro) or Indian. Although the Negroes, Coloreds and Indians together made up an overwhelming majority of the country's population, all were treated as inferiors by the English and Dutch Europeans and restrictive laws against them were in effect. Gandhi, accustomed to British domination of his own country, was shocked to discover that an even greater chasm separated white and colored peoples in South Africa.

Naturally it was the plight of the Indian people that interested Gandhi the most. Bit by bit he learned the history of his people in South Africa, finding that it was their diligence and business ability more than their failings that had aroused hostility to them. They had first come to South Africa in the 1860's, invited there by labor-hungry European planters under a system of indenture, a modified form of slavery. Receiving only meager board and lodging and a token salary, they were to work on the sugar and tea plantations for five years and at the end of that time they were to be given a choice between a paid passage back to India and the privilege of remaining in South Africa as free men. It was expected that those who chose to stay would become farmers and help to cultivate the vast untouched tracts of South African land. The freed Indians did a lot more than that. They prospered, first as farmers and then as landowners and businessmen. Merchants back in India heard of their success and came to South Africa to set up trade.

Dismayed by the influx of unwanted business competition, the white settlers began to notice and resent the differences between the Indians' way of life and their own. How ridiculous the Indians' religious customs were! Their standards of cleanliness, high in some respects, were painfully low in others. Their affluence, the Europeans thought, was due to nothing more than an unbusinesslike willingness to bargain with their customers. And there were entirely too many of these inferior "coolies." Something had to be done to stop the flow of Indians to South Africa.

Casting about for ways to discourage Indian settlement, the Europeans enacted laws and ordinances designed to keep Indians from coming to South Africa and to make life so difficult for those who were already there that they would give up and go back to their homeland. In the province of the Orange Free State Indians could work only at menial occupations; the province of Natal was in the process of enacting legislation that would impose a £3 tax on freed indentured servants who elected to stay in South Africa; Indians had to pay a £3 tax to enter the province of the Transvaal and, once in, they could neither vote nor own land nor even walk on the public footpaths.

Gandhi discovered that it was the practice of his Indian friends in Natal to "pocket" the insults they were constantly receiving. They pointed out that things were better for Indians in Natal than in the other provinces and they ran their lives and businesses within the restrictive framework imposed on them without complaining. Because he was planning to be in South Africa only a year, it didn't occur to Gandhi to do otherwise until, in the course of his legal business, he had to travel from Durban to Pretoria, the capital city of the Transvaal.

Gandhi bought a first-class train ticket and all went well until, at about nine o'clock in the evening, the train reached the city of Pietermaritzburg high up in the mountains. As the train stood in the station a white passenger came into the compartment where Gandhi was sitting and coolly looked him up and down. Then he went out and returned with three conductors. One of them informed Gandhi that he would have to leave the compartment and finish his journey in the luggage compartment.

"But I have a first-class ticket," Gandhi objected.

"That doesn't matter, you can't stay here," the conductor answered.

"I was allowed to travel in this compartment at Durban and I insist on my right to stay in it."

"No, you can't. If you don't leave I'll have to call a policeman to take you out."

"Go right ahead. I refuse to get out voluntarily."

The policeman was called and he took Gandhi by the arm and pulled him out of the first-class compartment. When he flatly refused to go to the rear compartment he and his luggage were unceremoniously dumped in the Maritzburg station and the train steamed away.

It was winter and the mountain air of Maritzburg was icy cold. Gandhi thought longingly of the overcoat in his suitcase but the station official had taken charge of his luggage and he didn't dare ask for it. He sat, shivering, in the deserted dark waiting room turning over in his mind the humiliating events that had left him stranded there. What should he do now? He was tempted to call off the whole South African venture and sail for home at once. He could, of course, stand on his rights as the holder of a first-class ticket, make a big fuss and demand apologies or he could, as Abdulla would advise, simply forget the incident and proceed on his way the next morning. All night long Gandhi huddled on the wooden bench in the waiting room and as the first light of dawn filtered through the dirt-streaked windows he made his decision. He would put aside his bitterness and stay in South Africa long enough to complete his legal assignment; while he was there he would fight as best he could the color prejudice that lay behind the insults he had received.

In Pretoria Gandhi was soon caught up in the legal business that had brought him. It was a complicated, challenging case, bringing him into contact with experienced lawyers from whom he began to learn the workaday, practical aspects of the law. He watched and listened and worked and as his knowledge grew he remembered his English friend's prophecy that industry and honesty would make an able lawyer of him. Slowly he began to find the self-confidence he had so sorely lacked.

Through business contacts Gandhi came to know several Englishmen in Pretoria. One of them, a lawyer and a lay preacher, befriended him and did his best to convert the young Indian to Christianity. Gandhi confessed that he still knew very little about Hinduism and explained that he must get to know his own religion thoroughly before thinking of embracing another. But his friend persisted and, moved by interest as well as by courtesy, Gandhi carefully read each religious book his friend gave him. Several other Christian friends also tried to convert him but all their efforts were in vain. Though deeply moved by the words of Jesus, Gandhi could not bring himself to believe that He was the only Incarnate Son of God. Nor did he think that Hinduism was a perfect faith; he couldn't accept its setting aside of certain people as "untouchables."

Confused about his religious beliefs, Gandhi began to read voraciously on the subjects of Christianity, Hinduism and Islam, the religion of Moslem Indians. Reading Leo Tolstoy's *The Kingdom of God Is Within You,* he was struck by the similarity between Tolstoy's insistence that God is to be found in every man and the basic philosophy of the Hindu scriptures. The power of love, said Tolstoy, is the most potent force on earth; the Gita said that ahimsa, the refusal to do harm and the duty to do good, is the highest virtue. Finally, Gandhi concluded that Hinduism allowed him the greatest latitude of religious belief and was, therefore, best for him. Nonetheless, he was very grateful to his Christian friends; they had, he told them, whetted his appetite for knowledge.

The memories of his humiliating experiences on the trip to Pretoria still rankled and Gandhi decided to act on his resolve to work for Indian rights. He called meetings of the Indians in Pretoria and urged them to form an association that would exert pressure on the government to treat them more fairly. After all, he pointed out, the British Empire was based on a Constitution that proclaimed racial equality for all its subjects. While it was true that Britain as a colonial power often debased its own ideals, in South Africa color prejudice had been legally recognized. Gandhi had no hope that the European emotional prejudice against colored peoples could be wiped out — he knew that fear of losing their power to a people who greatly outnumbered them lay behind their hostility to dark-skinned people — but he did think that the Indians could work toward erasing the color discrimination that was written into the laws.

The case which had brought Gandhi to Pretoria was settled out of court to the satisfaction of both parties and Gandhi returned to Durban to prepare for his voyage home to India. Just at that time the government of Natal announced that it was preparing a new bill which, if passed, would deny the vote to all the Indians in the province. Gandhi was indignant and at a farewell party given for him by his friends he urged the assembled guests to get together and fight the offensive bill. They would, they told him, if he would stay and help them. He agreed to stay on for another month.

Meetings were called, volunteers enrolled, money raised. In the excitement of taking action to secure their rights, all class and occupation distinctions among the Indians were forgotten and rich merchants worked side by side with lowly farmers. A petition was drawn up and it was published in the press with favorable comment. It was discussed in the House of Legislature, confounding those proponents of the bill who had argued that the absence of opposition from the Indians proved that they were unfit to vote. The original bill was eventually passed but by that time the Indian community was unified and committed to the fight for their legal rights. Their cause had received excellent publicity and the Indian people had been given invaluable training in the mechanics of political agitation. Again the question of Gandhi's return to India arose and again he was prevailed upon to stay, this time for an indefinite period.

4

The Durban Riot

Two SHIPS flying yellow flags lay at anchor in the port of Durban. On board 800 Indian men, women and children were showing the strain of having been cooped up for a long period of time. Petty grievances were aired, tempers flared, little children whined and tugged at their mothers' saris. They had all been at sea for eighteen days and now that they had reached South Africa they still had to stay on board the ships. The yellow flags fluttering from the masts signified that the ships were under quarantine. There had been plague in Bombay, the ships' port of departure, and the Durban medical authorities had ruled that the twenty-three days it took for cholera germs to incubate must pass before the passengers could disembark. On the crowded decks time passed slowly. The bigger children raced to and fro getting in everybody's way and when, from time to time, one would fall silent and sit quietly, his mother would anxiously press her hand to his forehead.

But was the quarantine the only reason the passengers were being kept on board? There were rumors going around that the people of Durban were hoping to keep the ships' passengers out of Natal even after the danger of cholera had passed.

Mohandas Gandhi was on board one of the ships. Six months earlier he had gone back to India to get his family and bring them to live with him in South Africa. The year that he had told Kasturbai he would be away had stretched to two and a half years and no end to his South African work was yet in sight.

Encouraging the Natal Indians to organize for effective political action Gandhi had helped them form the Natal Indian Congress for the purpose of exerting pressure on the South African government; hoping for widespread sympathy for the Indians' cause he had prepared carefully documented pamphlets outlining their grievances, which were distributed in India as well as in South Africa. Much had been done but the greater part of his task still lay ahead and Gandhi was anxious to have his family with him. While he was in India, he told his Natal associates, he would work to arouse Indian public opinion to the point where it would exert pressure on England. England might then insist that the South African authorities adhere more closely to the guarantees of racial equality contained in the British Constitution.

And so Gandhi had gone back to India in 1896 and for six months he had busied himself with visiting newspaper editors, writing reports and addressing public meetings. Again and again he spoke of the unhappy plight of the Indians in South Africa. Then at last he had gone home to Rajkot to supervise a flurry of last-minute shopping and packing and with Kasturbai, their two sons, Harilal, nine, and Manilal, five, and the ten-year-old son of his widowed sister, he had set sail again for South Africa.

Now, as the ship lay at anchor off Durban, Gandhi talked with the captain and a group of passengers about the Natal Indians' political situation. Kasturbai, unable to follow the thread of their discussions, looked out over the harbor and worried, not about the danger of cholera or about the talk of trouble ashore — she took a fatalistic attitude toward both — but about her own future. Across the choppy waters lay a strange land where she would have to set up housekeeping on her own without the guidance of the loving

mother and kind mother-in-law she missed so much already.
Of course she would be with her husband but after the long
separation he seemed almost a stranger to her. He was no
longer the shy, quiet boy who had left her three years before
to go to South Africa. Now he was a man, strong, self-
confident and wrapped up in his work. It was clear that he
would no longer brook any interference with his assuming
the role of lord and master. He would help her, he had said,
to become an "ideal wife" but it turned out that his help
was to consist of insisting that she do as he wished.

First there was the matter of dress. Deciding that his
status as leader of the Indian community in Natal would be
dimmed if his family arrived wearing their customary simple
Hindu clothes, Gandhi had decreed that Kasturbai and the
boys must all look "civilized." Shoes and stockings were the
order of the day for all and Kasturbai had to wear the Parsi
style sari that Gandhi believed would be more acceptable
in the cosmopolitan world of Durban than her own. Then
there was the technique of European table etiquette to be
mastered. As she struggled through her shipboard meals it
seemed to Kasturbai that the "civilized" knife and fork were
instruments of torture, cleverly designed to rob her of her
pleasure in eating. Her sons and nephew were no happier
about the Europeanizing process; they kept coming to her
with complaints of how their feet hurt in their shoes and
how confined their arms felt in their tight jackets. Harilal
and Manilal had discovered that complaining to Gandhi got
them nowhere — their new-found father, it appeared, could
be very stern. Kasturbai tried to soothe the boys; she hugged
them and gave them sweets and told them that if they were
patient, they would soon get used to the new clothes.

As the days of the quarantine passed, the rumors of a
storm brewing ashore came thick and fast. The white people

of Natal, the passengers learned, were seething with resentment against Gandhi. He had, they said, spread false reports in India about their inhumanity to the Indians in their country. They had heard that he had brought back two shiploads of people for the purpose of overrunning Natal with Indian immigrants. There was not a shred of truth in either of these contentions. Gandhi's public statements in India had been no more critical of South African whites than his speeches in South Africa had been; the only people he had persuaded to come back with him were his wife, his sons and his nephew. Yet, on shore, huge rallies were being held to inflame public opinion against him, and the ships' owners were being alternately besieged by bribes and threats with the object of inducing them to return their passengers to India.

Messages were sent to Gandhi aboard the ship, threatening him with violence if he dared to come ashore. Gandhi was calm. He assured the passengers that some way could be found to settle matters peacefully. He didn't believe that anything could be accomplished by force, he said. The captain asked him how he would stand by his principle of nonviolence if, once ashore, the whites carried out their violent threats. Gandhi answered that he hoped he would have the courage and good sense to forgive his attackers and to refrain from pressing charges against them. He was sure that they sincerely believed they were right and, therefore, he had no reason to be angry with them. The captain privately wondered if Gandhi would survive long enough to be as forgiving as he planned.

When the five-day quarantine period was over and the ships finally docked, it was suggested that Gandhi and his family leave their ship after dark in order to evade the enraged mob of waiting white people. But Gandhi felt that

Henry David Thoreau — a photographic portrait

Mohandas K. Gandhi as a law student

Gandhi with two of his workers sitting in front of his law office in Johannesburg.

A mounted Indian policeman rides down Gandhi's followers as they stage a protest raid on the government salt deposits at Dharasana.

it would be cowardly for him to sneak into Natal that way and, after ensuring his family's safe conduct to the house of a friend, he went ashore himself, determined to walk openly the distance of two miles to join them.

No sooner had he started up a street leading away from the dock than he was caught up in a swirling crowd of people who pelted him with stones, bricks and rotten eggs. His turban was snatched from his head and he was repeatedly kicked and beaten. As the mob closed in on him he clung to the front railing of a house and tried to stand his ground but he would certainly have been killed had it not been for the timely arrival of an English lady, the police superintendent's wife, who opened her parasol and bravely held it between the beleaguered Indian and the mob.

Hearing of the riot, the police superintendent sent a posse of men to escort Gandhi to his friend's house. The crowd of angry whites followed and surrounded the house, shouting their determination to get hold of Gandhi. The police superintendent, himself, arrived on the scene and, keeping the mob in check by bantering with them good-humoredly, he sent a message to Gandhi inside the house, advising him to make his escape in disguise. Gandhi hastily put on the uniform of an Indian constable and, in the company of a detective, he left the house by a side door, slipped unrecognized through the crowd and took refuge in the police station while the police superintendent distracted the mob by singing with them, "Hang old Gandhi on the sour apple tree."

News of the incident reached England and the Secretary of State for the Colonies demanded that the government of Natal prosecute Gandhi's assailants. But Gandhi refused to press charges. "I do not want to bring anyone to book," he said. "I am sure that when the truth becomes known they

will be sorry for their conduct." He had guessed correctly.
When newspaper reporters interviewed him and then
printed the true story of his return to Africa, there was a
great deal of shame felt in the European community.
Gandhi's forgiving attitude toward his attackers was wondered at and greatly admired.

Now came a relatively quiet time in Gandhi's life. Congress affairs claimed most of his attention but he was concerned with domestic matters as well. Soon after getting
settled in her new home Kasturbai gave birth to a third
son, Ramdas, and though Gandhi engaged a nurse, her
duties were largely confined to caring for Kasturbai, for
Gandhi insisted on taking on most of the care of the baby
himself until Kasturbai was strong enough to take over.

Next he turned to the problem of the education of his sons
and nephew. The schools attended by the European children were out of the question, for they did not welcome
Indians and the teaching in the mission schools for non-
Europeans was woefully inadequate. Gandhi tried teaching
the boys himself only to find it impossible to devote enough
time to the task. An English governess was engaged but
she did not live up to expectations. In the end, the boys'
formal education was neglected. They stayed at home,
learning as best they could in the "school of experience"
that Gandhi had concluded was best for them.

Relations between Kasturbai and her husband still left a
a great deal to be desired. Gandhi was ever hopeful about
making Kasturbai into "an ideal wife," one who would cheerfully adjust herself to his way of life, but Kasturbai found
his way of life very difficult to take. Gandhi was extraor-
dinarily hospitable and kept inviting law clerks from his
office and his associates in Indian civic affairs to come and

live with his family for extended periods of time and the presence of strangers in her home, strangers who were urged to make themselves part of the family, was very hard on the young woman who had come straight from a carefully secluded and tightly knit Hindu family life. Far from home, amidst people whose customs were very different from those she had known, she was distinctly ill at ease and painfully homesick.

Then, too, Gandhi's standards for her conduct sometimes seemed unattainably high; not only did she have to put up with the inconvenience of a constant stream of guests, but she also had to do the most menial chores connected with the care of their rooms. There was no indoor plumbing in their house and consequently one of the daily household tasks was the emptying of the chamber pots used by the family and the guests. Gandhi would not ask their servant to do this job, preferring to do it himself with Kasturbai's assistance. Once, when she rebelled against cleaning the room of an untouchable visitor, Gandhi lost his temper and tried to push her out of the gate of their house. She wept and pleaded with him and he finally relented. "I was a cruelly kind husband," Gandhi said in his autobiography. "I regarded myself as her teacher, and so harassed her out of my blind love for her."

There were further adjustments in store for Kasturbai. Gandhi decided that the style in which they were living was unnecessarily grand and that expenses should be cut down. The laundryman's bill bore the brunt of the first attack. Gandhi announced that he would study the art of washing and then teach it to Kasturbai. The first collar Gandhi washed and ironed was badly overstarched and made him the object of great merriment in court when the starch flaked off the collar, covering his shoulders with white dust. Barbering was Gandhi's next venture. An English barber had refused to cut his hair because his skin was brown so Gandhi did it himself. He did well enough with the front but he botched the job on the back of his head and his fellow lawyers shook with laughter again.

On the outbreak of the Boer War, a conflict between the British and Dutch settlers of South Africa, Gandhi organized an all-Indian ambulance corps to work on the British side despite the fact that his sympathies were with the Boers. He was sure that in spite of flagrant abuses of its power, the British Empire was a beneficent influence on the world and he reasoned that South African Indians fighting for their rights as British subjects should be ready to assume their obligations to the Empire. The valiant work of the ambulance corps gave the lie to the general impression that Indians were cowardly and made many friends for the Indian people. Unfortunately, this friendship was not reflected in any inclination to amend the inequitable laws.

In 1901 Gandhi felt that he could safely leave the Natal Indian Congress in the hands of the young men who had been trained as leaders under his tutelage. He wanted to go back to India to practice law and to work in the political arena there. The Indian community agreed to let him go only upon receiving his promise that he would return immediately if an unexpected situation arose and he was needed.

The Gandhi family did not stay in India long. No sooner had Gandhi settled down to a successful law practice in Bombay than he was called back to South Africa. The Indian situation had worsened, especially in the province of the Transvaal. He must come there at once.

Hoping to return soon Gandhi left his family in Bombay but within a year he had sent for them. He didn't know when he could come back to India and he wanted them with him. So Kasturbai sailed for South Africa again and joined Gandhi in the city of Johannesburg in the Transvaal. Harilal stayed behind in Bombay; he was to finish high school there before joining the rest of the family.

5

The Gentle Tyrant

WHEN GANDHI came across an idea that appealed to him, an approach to life that seemed to bring him closer to the truth, he immediately made it a part of his own philosophy. When, in 1904, he read John Ruskin's book *Unto This Last,* he said that his life was "transformed" and it wasn't long before Kasturbai and the Gandhi boys found that Ruskin's theories had transformed their lives as well.

Ruskin believed that a man's best chance for happiness lay in working in cooperation with other men to improve the society in which he lived; he advocated a rejection of the luxuries of civilization and a return to simplicity. Reading Ruskin's book, Gandhi suddenly decided that ". . . the life of the tiller of the soil and the handicraftsman is the life worth living," and he determined to translate his beliefs into action.

Soon after his return to Africa Gandhi had started a weekly magazine, *Indian Opinion,* and he used its columns to explain to his readers the principles underlying the Indians' fight for freedom. Now, under the influence of Ruskin's book, he persuaded some wealthy friends to help him buy a farm near Phoenix, fourteen miles from Durban, and he moved the presses of *Indian Opinion* there. He was sure that at Phoenix he and his family and associates could lead the cooperative life that Ruskin recommended, relying on their own manual labor to produce their food and other necessities of life. He couldn't afford to give up his law practice entirely and retire to Phoenix so he and Kasturbai and their sons divided their time between the farm and their new home in Johannesburg.

Ruskin's ghost haunted Kasturbai in both places. Gandhi interfered in every detail of the management of the household, insisting on what Kasturbai must have considered to be outlandish simplicity. Ordinary packaged sugar was an unnecessary luxury, Gandhi said, and when Kasturbai's cooking recipes called for sweetening, raw sugar had to do. Spices and seasonings became taboo and bread could no longer be bought from the baker but had to be baked at home of hand-ground flour. The flour-grinding chores were apportioned among the Gandhi family and the ranks of the ever-present guests, but most of the time Kasturbai managed to avoid any share in that particular job; in his autobiography Gandhi noted that "the grinding hour was her usual time for commencing kitchen work." The Gandhis still had a servant, but since everyone was expected to work hard and no one was allowed to turn up his nose at menial tasks, he was scarcely distinguishable from the rest of the family. The "school of experience" that the Gandhi boys attended assigned them the responsibility for emptying the chamber pots.

What a pity it was that Gandhi could not see that he was making his wife and sons miserable! Kasturbai, he reasoned, should be happy to accompany him on his search for the highest truths, but he overlooked the lesser truth that, intellectually, he had far outpaced her and, emotionally, he had deserted her. To Kasturbai, unable even to read or write, the philosophies of Tolstoy and Ruskin, her husband's guiding geniuses, meant only increased drudgery for her; her marriage had turned out to be not the easy existence of an ordinary Indian lawyer's wife, but a matter of running a hotel under the most primitive conditions with the innkeeper constantly at her elbow.

Denying his sons all the normal pleasures and privileges of boyhood, Gandhi offered them only the rewards of hard work. The younger boys kept their noses to the flour-grinding stone when Gandhi was nearby and scampered off to play between times, but Harilal, the oldest son, balked when he discovered that his father planned a future for him made up of equal parts of manual labor and self-denial.

When he finished high school in Bombay and returned to South Africa, Harilal saw his dreams of a business career or a profession go up in the smoke of his father's flat assertion that further formal schooling would be a waste of time. How, Harilal wanted to know, was he to earn a living? Hadn't Gandhi himself enjoyed the advantages of an English legal education? It was no use — by that time Gandhi had decided that his own legal training had hindered rather than aided him in his life work. If Harilal learned to work with his hands and dedicated himself to service he'd have no trouble earning his bread. The subject was closed. Feeling cheated and misunderstood, Harilal was ripe to fall in love but here, too, he ran afoul of his father's unyielding convictions. Gandhi thought of his own child marriage as a near disaster. He still shuddered when he remembered how he had tormented Kasturbai with his youthful jealousy and lust; how yearnings to be with his lovely child-bride had kept him from his dying father's side. No, his sons must be mature men before they took brides. Marriage, Gandhi said, was out of the question for Harilal for the time being. Frustrated at every turn, Harilal sulked and finally consoled himself by marrying secretly. The secret was soon out and Gandhi was righteously enraged; Harilal had not only married against his father's wishes but he had cheated his parents of their prerogative of choosing their daughter-in-law. For a time Gandhi would have nothing to do with either Harilal or his wife, but when a daughter was born to them, bygones were allowed to be bygones and Harilal, his wife, Gulab, and their little girl, Rami, were invited to join the discipline and service brigade at Phoenix Farm.

Gandhi loved his wife and sons but he ruled them with the iron rod of his "moral force." Compassionate and understanding of everyone else's human failings, he would accept nothing less than perfection from them. He not only set them firmly on the path to goals that he had picked out for them, but he prodded them when they faltered on the journey and dictated what they were to eat and wear en route.

Gandhi's family took part in his medical as well as his spiritual "experiments with the truth." Normally they had only to submit to the various fruit diets and mudpacks on the abdomen that he believed were beneficial to their health, but on several occasions he took one or another of their lives out of the hands of the medical profession and into his own. When Manilal was ten years old and desperately ill with typhoid complicated by pneumonia, his doctor prescribed a strengthening diet of eggs and beef broth as the best possible medicine. Gandhi objected on the basis of his vegetarian beliefs. The doctor was indignant; other Hindus, he said, were able to make compromises with their religious convictions when their children's lives were at stake. But Gandhi stood firm and calmly replied, "Even for life itself we may not do certain things." Gandhi's persuasive charm must have worked on even that most outraged of men — a doctor whose medical advice has been rejected by a layman — for when Gandhi announced that he would take on the main responsibility for Manilal's care himself and asked the doctor to look in on the boy from time to time to check on his progress, the doctor agreed.

Gandhi nursed the sick boy day and night, giving him frequent hip baths, feeding him orange juice diluted with water, and praying. One night Manilal's temperature reached 104 degrees and the boy tossed hot and sleepless on his bed. Hoping to induce the perspiration that would bring the fever down, Gandhi carefully wrapped his son in a wet sheet and covered him with blankets. Then, worried and restless, he left Manilal in his mother's care and went out for a walk to wrestle with his doubts about whether or not he had done the right thing in scorning the doctor's advice. As soon as he returned Manilal called out to him, plaintively asking to be taken out of the blankets. Gandhi felt the boy's forehead. It was wet with perspiration. Relief flooding over him, he said to the sick boy, "Manilal, your fever is sure to go now. A little more perspiration and I will take you out." Sick as he was, Manilal found the strength to resist. "Please take me out of this furnace," he pleaded. "You can wrap me up again later if you like." Gandhi managed to keep him in the wet pack a few more minutes by distracting his attention and then, as the perspiration streamed down the boy's forehead, his father undid the pack and tenderly dried Manilal's body. The burning heat had gone; the fever had broken; Manilal would get well. Father and son fell asleep on the same bed.

Gandhi "doctored" Kasturbai, too, whenever he got the chance. When, in 1900, she gave birth to their fourth son, Devadas, unexpectedly early and there was no time to fetch medical aid, Gandhi confidently delivered the baby himself.

Once, when Kasturbai suffered a setback after an operation, Gandhi decided that she would recuperate faster if she stopped using salt on her food and gave up eating pulse, a vegetable both he and she loved. Kasturbai objected and impulsively accused her husband of wanting to deny her pleasures that he couldn't deny himself. No sooner were the words out of her mouth than she was sorry she had said them. To prove his love for her, he immediately vowed to do without salt and pulse for a year whether or not she gave them up. Kasturbai was heartbroken; Gandhi had so little pleasure as it was and now she had goaded him into another sacrifice. She promised to give up the disputed delicacies and begged him to take back his vow. He told her that he could not possibly retract a vow and, weeping, Kasturbai wailed, "You are too obstinate. You will listen to none." There could be no doubt about it: Gandhi, the husband and father, was an unyielding tyrant but, almost always, his was a very gentle tyranny.

Salt, spices, refined sugar, bakery bread — all these had disappeared from the family table either because Gandhi considered them luxuries or because he thought they were unhealthful, but when it came to his own diet, Gandhi was most interested in the effect of his food on his spiritual well-being. He had consciously set out to attain the state of desirelessness prescribed by the Gita and the self-restraint recommended by Ruskin and, deciding that "passion in man is generally coexistent with a hankering after the pleasures of the palate," he decided to discipline his passions by frequent fasts. Between times he ate only fruits, nuts and grains. But desirelessness evaded him — the fasting only served to increase his appetite and, try as he might, he could not help looking forward to the simple meals he allowed himself. He refused, however, to be discouraged. The annoying persistence of his appetite only proved to him that his mental attitude was not yet all that it might be and he consoled himself by remembering a certain verse from the Gita:

> *For a man who is fasting his senses*
> *Outwardly, the sense-objects disappear,*
> *Leaving the yearning behind; but when*
> *He has seen the Highest,*
> *Even the yearning disappears.*

In 1906 Gandhi took the final step in his search for the "Highest." He vowed to observe *brahmacharya*, complete chastity, for the rest of his life. Restraint, simplicity, strong moral purpose. These were Gandhi's guideposts; he was "in training" for the tremendous spiritual and physical trials that lay ahead of him.

6

Satyagraha

PETITIONS AND propaganda were the Indians' only weapons during the first thirteen years of their fight for legal equality in South Africa. But, in 1906, the Transvaal government provoked them into open defiance of the law.

A new ordinance was proposed that would, if it were adopted, require each Indian in the Transvaal to register with the authorities, be fingerprinted and carry an identifying certificate with him at all times. An Indian caught without his certificate would be jailed or deported. Indians in every walk of life were outraged; fingerprinting had heretofore been reserved for criminals and the necessity of carrying a "pass" seemed an unbearable humiliation. The proposed law was promptly dubbed "The Black Act" and an aroused Indian community held a mass meeting to consider what could be done to combat it.

At the meeting it was suggested that every Indian pledge himself to participate in a campaign of deliberate disobedience if the law was passed. Gandhi, looking out over the audience of excited, indignant people, was thrilled at the idea of effective protest and, at the same time, troubled. He wondered if the Indian people, at the moment filled with enthusiasm for their cause, had the stamina to take the consequences of lawbreaking. Government reprisals would surely be harsh and the Indian protest would be laughed out of existence if, having vowed to resist, the Indians broke their vow and gave in. He decided not to mince words and, addressing the meeting, he warned the assembled Indians that if they defied the Black Act they might well face not only jail and deportation but hard labor, floggings, attachment of property and heavy fines as well. "In short," he concluded, ". . . it is not at all impossible that we might have to endure every hardship that we can imagine, and wisdom lies in pledging ourselves on the understanding that we shall have to suffer all that and worse." Undismayed, his audience unanimously vowed to resist the proposed law.

Having decided on active resistance to repressive legislation, the Indian protest now needed a name. It had been called passive resistance but the word "passive" was taken by many to mean inactive and thus the term was not truly descriptive. It was finally decided that *satyagraha,* a combination of two Indian words, best described the idea that Gandhi felt lay behind the movement. *Satya* means "truth" or "love," and *agraha* means "force"; *satyagraha* means "the force contained in truth and love," or "nonviolent resistance."

The Satyagraha philosophy made a clear distinction between the sin and the sinner. The Satyagrahi, Gandhi said, hates the sin but, believing his opponent to have temporarily strayed from the path of justice, he continues to feel kindly disposed toward the sinner and tries hard to understand his point of view. Wanting neither to defeat nor to punish his opponent he works toward compromise with him. He willingly accepts the consequences of his actions, whether they are imprisonment or physical injury or economic reprisal, certain that his suffering will afflict the conscience of his opponent. Those who practice satyagraha, Gandhi pointed out, must be good citizens who normally obey all the laws of the state; by deliberately breaking one law, while continuing to abide by all the others, they spotlight their conviction that that one law is flagrantly unjust and in conflict with the higher law of conscience. Summing up the revolutionary idea that lay behind his revolutionary approach to politics, Gandhi called nonviolent resistance an "all-sided sword" that "blesses him who uses it and him against whom it is used, without drawing a drop of blood . . ."

In 1907 the Black Act passed into law and the Satyagraha movement swung into action. The authorities were dismayed to find only a small number of Indians presenting themselves for registration and, angered, they arrested Gandhi and several other Satyagrahis. Gandhi was given a two-month sentence thus inaugurating for him an almost lifelong career of jail-going in the interests of Indian freedom. He was overjoyed to find that each day more and more Indians, picked up for refusing to register, were joining him; the jail was becoming badly overcrowded. As he was to do so often in the years ahead, Gandhi passed his time happily in prison by indulging in an orgy of reading. There wasn't time in his busy ordinary life for books, and prison was an ideal place to continue his self-assigned study of religion, philosophy and history. Conditions in jail were far from pleasant but Gandhi, his nose buried in a book, hardly noticed.

While Gandhi read, the Transvaal authorities paced the floor. The little Indian had put them in an unprecedented spot. Heretofore, making an example of a few lawbreakers by firmly jailing them had always served as an ample warning to others who might contemplate following in their footsteps. But such had been far from the case this time. Indeed, the jailing of Gandhi and four other Satyagrahis had had quite the opposite effect from that intended. The imprisoned men were obviously serving not as a warning but as an inspiration to their countrymen! It was a most embarrassing situation — one that called for an immediate change in tactics.

Before three weeks of his sentence had passed Gandhi was summoned to a conference with General Jan Christiaan Smuts, South Africa's Minister of Finance and Defense. Smuts told Gandhi that the government's main object in requiring Indian registration was to obtain a census of the Indian population in the Transvaal and he promised that if Indians would register voluntarily, he would take steps to repeal the Black Act. Gandhi agreed to the compromise and he and the other Indian prisoners were promptly released.

A storm of protests from his fellow workers greeted Gandhi on his return to Johannesburg. Why had he agreed to a half measure? they wanted to know. What was to prevent General Smuts from going back on his word? Attempting to still the uproar, Gandhi pointed out that fighting with satyagraha depended on faith in the basic goodness of one's opponent, in the eventual triumph of his conscience over his desire to do evil. "A Satyagrahi bids goodbye to fear," he said. "He is therefore never afraid of trusting the opponent. Even if the opponent plays him false twenty times, the Satyagrahi is ready to trust him for the twenty-first time."

Gandhi tried to convince his countrymen that their best interests would be served by presenting themselves voluntarily for registration and he announced that he would be the first to do so. But some of the Indians were so positive that he had betrayed their cause that when he started out for the registration office several of them waylaid him and beat and kicked him unmercifully. Gandhi fainted and only the appearance of some European passers-by saved his life. He was carried to the home of a missionary friend and there, in spite of considerable pain and weakness, he insisted that the Registrar of Asiatics be sent for; he was still determined to be the first Indian to register and be fingerprinted. His attackers were caught but again Gandhi would not press charges. "They thought that I was doing what was wrong," he explained to his friends. ". . . I therefore request that no steps be taken against them." On his recovery he urged the Indians over and over again to register and to thereby fulfill their end of the bargain. Most of the Indians allowed themselves to be convinced.

But, General Smuts broke his word; he made no attempt to repeal the Black Act and the resentful Indian community prepared to take steps. Because honesty was to be the keystone of the whole Satyagraha struggle, Gandhi insisted on warning the government of the action planned. Accordingly, notice was given that if a decision to repeal the hated Act had not been taken by August 16, 1908, the Indian registration certificates would be collected and burned! Gandhi, by now a practiced politician, was fully aware of the value of a bit of drama in unifying a fighting force and in pinpointing the public's attention on a specific issue.

A huge public meeting was held on the appointed day. At the last minute word was received from the government to the effect that it was unable to change the course of its action. Then two thousand registration certificates were collected from the outstretched hands of the assembled cheering Indians, thrown into a large iron cauldron and, when someone shouted "Light it, Gandhi," set ablaze. Representatives of the European press attending the meeting were awed by the scene. The Indian community was now in open rebellion against the government.

7

Gandhi and Thoreau

GANDHI WAS in jail again. He and several other Satyagrahis had taken part in a series of illegal border crossings to test whether the government would put teeth into its restrictive legislation. The authorities had immediately demonstrated that they meant business; all the Satyagrahis were arrested. On October 10, 1908, Gandhi was given a choice between serving a two-month sentence and paying a fine of £25. He chose to serve his sentence and it was during this second term in jail that he first came across Henry Thoreau's prescription for "peaceable revolution." Ironically, it was in the prison library that Gandhi found Thoreau's essay "Civil Disobedience."

Gandhi was thrilled when he saw the very principles for which he had been fighting, to which he had dedicated his life, set forth so stirringly in the words of the young American rebel. Thoreau, in a Massachusetts jail, believed that "Under a government which imprisons any unjustly, the true place for a just man is also a prison"; Gandhi, in jail in the Transvaal, heartily agreed. Both men considered themselves patriots. Each believed that in deliberately breaking an unjust law he was performing a service to the state he loved. By refusing to be a party to Massachusetts's support of the Mexican War and the Fugitive Slave Law, Thoreau tried to demonstrate to his state that it was running counter to the ideals of American justice; Gandhi, a loyal British subject, broke only those laws of the South African government which were inconsistent with the higher laws of the British

Empire. The circumstances of their struggles were different, the underlying principle was the same.

Thoreau had said that a group, sure of the justice of its cause, and ceasing to conform to the will of those in power, is "irresistible when it clogs by its whole weight" and Gandhi found the words directly applicable to the Satyagraha movement. South African Indians, determined to stop "pocketing" the insults they received and acting together, could clog the machinery of the unjust government. By filling South African jails to overflowing they could embarrass the authorities and, by the spectacle of their suffering, they would appeal to the consciences of their opponents.

So separately placed in time and space, Thoreau and Gandhi met in their ideas. How different these two men were, yet, how much the same. Thoreau was a poet; Gandhi, a man of action — yet each guided his life according to the same set of principles. Certainly, the fact that both had studied the ancient Eastern philosophies accounts for some of the similarity between them.

Right action, harmlessness, desirelessness — these the Bhagavad-Gita prescribes to help man in his difficult ascent to Brahman, the truth that lies within himself. Right action was for Thoreau the obligation "to do at any time what I think right"; for Gandhi, tempted to run away from the harsh South African discrimination against Indians, it was the decision to stay and fight the evil of color prejudice without counting the cost. Harmlessness meant to Thoreau leaving his cherished solitude and defying the state because he could not bear to watch his tax dollars used to kill or unjustly imprison men who had done him no harm; Gandhi, making of ahimsa a whole way of life, insisted on loving his European opponents while fighting the evil in their system of government. Both men schooled themselves to want and to need little. In the woods around Walden Pond, Thoreau sang the praises of hard work, a simple diet and self-restraint; Gandhi not only followed this regimen himself but was surprisingly successful in convincing everyone around him to do the same. The precepts of the Gita, first put into writing more than twenty-five centuries ago, are echoed in the poetry of Thoreau's philosophy and re-echoed in the poetry of Gandhi's life.

Thoreau and Gandhi were both religious men, yet each was critical of the religion into which he had been born. The Concord rebel refused to accept the restrictions of any religious dogma; Gandhi, accepting the Hindu faith because it demanded so little of him, blandly rejected its concept of untouchability as offensive to his idea of religion.

Sitting in his cell in Volksrust Prison in the Transvaal, Gandhi wrote an article for *Indian Opinion* on the value of going to jail for a cause and, moved by the power and the beauty of Thoreau's account of his rebellion against an evil system, he ended his own essay with this quotation from "Civil Disobedience":

> . . . I saw that, if there was a wall of stone between me and my townsmen, there was a still more difficult one to climb or break through before they could get to be as free as I was. I did not for a moment feel confined, and the walls seemed a great waste of stone and mortar. I felt as if I alone of all my townsmen had paid my tax. They plainly did not know how to treat me, but behaved like persons who are underbred. In every threat and in every compliment there was a blunder; for they thought that my chief desire was to stand the other side of that stone wall. I could not but smile to see how industriously they locked the door

on my meditations, which followed them out again without let or hindrance, and *they* were really all that was dangerous. As they could not reach me, they had resolved to punish my body; just as boys, if they cannot come at some person against whom they have a spite, will abuse his dog. I saw that the State was half-witted, that it was timid as a lone woman with her silver spoons, and that it did not know its friends from its foes, and I lost all my remaining respect for it, and pitied it.

Thoreau, the poet; Gandhi, the politician — Thoreau, a white American; Gandhi, a brown-skinned Indian. Externally, they were worlds apart, yet they were, in fact, brothers related by ties that unite all men who search through a world of illusion for truth. Both were resolved to defy injustice regardless of the cost; each was committed to a nonviolent assault on the conscience of his mighty opponent. On a shelf in the prison library Gandhi found new strength for his struggle against the authorities who had imprisoned him. Satyagraha in South Africa was Thoreau's peaceable revolution transplanted and enlarged.

8

The Great March

THE SOUTH AFRICAN Indians' dissatisfaction became a matter of wider and wider concern. All over India, large amounts of money were collected for the Satyagrahis in Africa. In England, those with a liberal point of view were distressed by the Empire's sanction of color discrimination, others feared the rumblings of discontent in the Indian colony. The cables between England and South Africa hummed with heated arguments. Conferences were held and attempts were made to reconcile the opposing factions. But the South African authorities would not admit the legal equality of Indians and Europeans, and the Satyagrahis were determined to press for their rights. It was obvious that another battle would be joined.

To prepare for the struggle ahead Gandhi and his co-workers established a sanctuary for the families of Satyagraha workers who were sure to be imprisoned during the course of the protest. A European friend of the Indians donated a tract of land near Johannesburg and Gandhi named it Tolstoy Farm, dedicating it to service and simplicity. The population of the Farm varied according to the number of Satyagrahis in jail. While in residence there everyone lived a life reduced to its barest essentials in deference to Gandhi's belief that only through the control of his bodily desires could the promise of man's spirit be fulfilled.

The routine followed at the Farm was spartan. Everyone slept wrapped in blankets on the ground, got up early, worked at digging, hoeing, spinning and flour-grinding all day, and retired soon after dark. Gandhi announced that meat would be served to those who did not share his fervor for vegetarianism, but he was very pleased when all decided to join him in a meatless diet. Alcohol and tobacco were forbidden. Gandhi considered the people at Tolstoy Farm his family and he kept a stern though loving father's eye on one and all. Sometimes the children disappointed him; there were times when their attention strayed from the joys of hard labor. Speaking of them, Gandhi said:

> . . . They took delight in the work, and so they did not generally need any other exercise or games. Of course some of them, and sometimes all of them, malingered or shirked. Sometimes I connived at their pranks, but often I was strict with them . . . Whenever I was strict, I would, by argument, convince them that it was not right to play with one's work. The conviction would, however, be short-lived, the next moment they would again leave their work and go to play.

Undismayed by these occasional lapses, Gandhi looked for the brighter side of the situation and ruefully commented, "All the same we got along and at any rate they built up fine physiques."

Pressure on the government by the Satyagrahis continued and, in 1912, the Indians rejoiced at what they believed was a great government concession to Indian equality. The authorities assured them that a lifting of the color ban on immigration was planned and that the £3 tax on freed indentured servants would be repealed. However, cold water was again thrown on Indian hopes when Smuts retracted the promise given, saying that pressure from the European settlers would not permit him to lift the tax. The next year the government added coals to the fire of Indian resentment when it announced that from that time forward only Christian marriages would be considered legal in South Africa. In imposing this most humiliating restraint of all, the government had gone too far; the Satyagrahis swung into action.

As an opening move in a campaign of deliberate disobedience, a group of women volunteers illegally crossed the border from Natal into the Transvaal while another group of women crossed from the Transvaal into Natal. Those entering the Transvaal were promptly arrested and the other group, finding themselves still free, persuaded a group of Indian coal-miners at the city of Newcastle to go out on strike. The women were then jailed and the miners' strike grew. Soon thousands of strikers had assembled in Newcastle, eager for leadership.

Since the Satyagrahis were aiming to be arrested in order to focus attention on the injustice of the law, Gandhi decided to place the responsibility for feeding and housing the multitude of miners on the government jails. He told the strikers of his plans for them and tried to discourage those whose zeal was uncertain by reminding them of the miserable conditions they would encounter in jail. The picture he painted was very black indeed but the miners would not be dissuaded and on October 13, 1913, between five and six thousand men started out for the city of Charlestown, situated on the Natal-Transvaal border thirty-six miles away.

In Charlestown Gandhi telephoned a message to General Smuts informing him that the marchers intended to cross the border illegally in protest against the humiliating restrictions imposed on them. They would, Gandhi added, call off the march if the government promised to lift the tax. While Gandhi held the phone, Smuts's secretary gave the General the message and, in less than a minute, she returned to say, "General Smuts will have nothing to do with you. You may do just as you please." The march would go on as planned.

Every attempt had been made to make the Satyagrahis' position clear. When a group of angry white people announced that they intended to turn the Indians back at the border by force, a European friend of Gandhi's pleaded with them to try to understand what the Indians were trying to do and said:

> . . . They do not wish to fight with you or to fill the country . . . They propose to enter the Transvaal not with a view to settle there, but only as an effective demonstration against the unjust tax which is levied on them. They are brave men. They will not injure you in person or in property, they will not fight with you, but enter the Transvaal they will, even in the face of your gunfire . . . They propose to melt, and I know they will melt, your hearts by self-suffering.

On November 6, 1913, the "invasion" commenced. The ragged column of marchers advanced eight miles into the Transvaal before the authorities took action. Gandhi was arrested by a few unarmed officials and he considered the fact that they faced his huge "army" unafraid "a testimony of merit the government of South Africa gave to the movement." He transferred the leadership of the march to a trusted associate, with the instructions that the demonstrators were to continue toward Tolstoy Farm as best they could. He was soon released on bail and he hurried back to lead his army. He was arrested twice more. The third time he was not allowed release on bail and the marchers straggled on without him. However, before they reached their destination the government rounded them up, packed them into railroad cars, and deported them out of the Transvaal and back to Natal. Gandhi was brought to trial and sentenced to three months in jail.

When the striking miners were forcibly returned to Natal and imprisoned under shocking conditions, news of their plight aroused a furor of protests overseas in India and in England. Now huge amounts of money poured in from India to support the resistance movement. Approximately fifty thousand indentured laborers went out on strike in sympathy with the striking miners. The Transvaal authorities, under strong pressure from England, appointed a commission to investigate the Indians' complaints and freed Gandhi and the other imprisoned Indian leaders.

Gandhi had good reason to doubt the integrity of the commission and demanded that it include some men friendly to the Indian cause. His demand was refused and he informed the government that the Indians planned another mass march on the first day of the new year. But, before long, a new development caused Gandhi to announce an electrifying change of plans. The white employees of the South African railroads had called a nationwide strike because of grievances of their own and Gandhi promptly called off the projected Indian march. He explained that the Satyagrahis did not want to take advantage of the government while it was trying to cope with the difficult situation brought on by the railroad strike. Every European in South Africa thought Gandhi must be out of his senses. This was going against all the rules of political warfare: if one had hopes of winning the game of politics one simply did not stand aside when one's opponent was down and wait for him to get up before attacking him again. It wasn't "smart" but it worked well for the Indians. Gandhi's dramatic generosity won the Indians many new friends and appreciably relaxed the tensions between the opposing parties.

Again Smuts summoned Gandhi to a conference and the Dutch general and the little Indian bargained long and hard. Each was determined to do his best for his own cause but, by this time, each respected the other and, most important, each was willing to compromise. Gandhi had always aimed at compromise and Smuts had come to the conclusion that it was simply too impractical for the government authorities to put twenty thousand determined Indians in jail. After a long series of talks between the two men it was announced that a settlement had been reached. The Smuts-Gandhi agreement provided that (1) Indian marriages would henceforth be considered legal, (2) the £3 tax on freed indentured Indian laborers would be lifted and (3) Indian indentured-servant immigration from India would cease by 1920.

It was only a partial victory for the Indians; Gandhi never claimed that it was more than that, but he believed that it was a significant step toward eventual legal equality of white and nonwhite people in South Africa. "Nurse the settlement," he urged his followers. "See to it that the promises made are carried out. . . . Zealously remove all causes which we may have given for the rise and growth of anti-Indian prejudice . . . and patiently cultivate and inform European opinion so as to enable the government of the day . . . to restore to us our rights."

Now, with the winning of substantial concessions from the South African government, Gandhi felt sure that the South African phase of his struggle had ended. His duty now lay in India, a land that he felt he hardly knew. Turning over the leadership of the Satyagraha movement to well-trained associates and parting sadly from his friends and co-workers, Gandhi sailed with his family for India in July of 1914.

Before leaving Africa, Gandhi sent a pair of slippers he had made in prison to his long-time adversary, General Jan Christiaan Smuts. Twenty-five years later, on the occasion of Gandhi's seventieth birthday, Smuts spoke of the Gandhi he had known:

> . . . It was my fate to be the antagonist of a man for whom even then I had the highest respect . . . He never forgot the human background of the situation, never lost his temper or succumbed to hatred, and preserved his gentle humor even in the most trying situations. His manner and spirit . . . contrasted markedly with the ruthless and brutal forcefulness which is the vogue in our day. . . .

In the course of the intervening years Smuts had not forgotten what a source of irritation Gandhi had been to him:

> . . . I must freely admit that his activities at that time were very trying to me . . . His method was deliberately to break the law, and to organize his followers into a mass movement . . . In both provinces a wild and disconcerting commotion was created, large numbers of Indians had to be imprisoned for lawless behavior, and Gandhi himself received — what no doubt he desired — a period of rest and quiet in jail. For him everything went according to plan. For me — the defender of law and order — there was the usual trying situation, the odium of carrying out a law which had not strong public support, and finally the discomfiture when the law was repealed.

Referring to the sandals which Gandhi had sent him, Smuts added, "I have worn these sandals for many a summer . . .

even though I may feel that I am not worthy to stand in the shoes of so great a man."

Though his greatest battles lay ahead of him in India, South Africa had been the crucible in which the character of Gandhi the warrior was fired. He had arrived in Durban a young man, untested, unsure of himself and yearning for material success. What an unlikely soil for the seeds of greatness! Yet, under this man's leadership, the Indian people in South Africa, once apathetic about the snowballing denial of their rights, rallied and found unity, courage and a sense of purpose. Following Mohandas Gandhi, 2700 Indians had gone willingly to jail and, as a direct result of his efforts, a repressive and authoritarian government had relented and given important legal rights to the Indian minority it had feared. Gandhi's uncompromising honesty and his lack of animosity toward those who sought to crush him had won him the respect of friend and foe alike.

What had happened to the man himself? Where had he found the enormous reserves of courage that enabled him to lead a powerless minority to victory? His own humiliating experiences with the color bar were at the root of it all. Jolted out of his placid acceptance of the white-master principle, Gandhi dedicated himself to a cause and, almost overnight, the ordinary young Indian lawyer became a compelling leader.

In the dark of the Maritzburg railroad station he had set his course — duty and truth. His reading, particularly the works of John Ruskin and Leo Tolstoy, had strengthened his own convictions about the perfectability of man and the virtues of simplicity and self-reliance. Searching for truth he had studied religions and had come to believe that all were parts of one universal religion; in the words of Jesus he heard echoed the precepts of harmlessness and the power of love written in his cherished Bhagavad-Gita. In Henry Thoreau he had found a spiritual brother; Thoreau's credo, "The only obligation which I have a right to assume is to do at any time what I think right," was Gandhi's own. He freely acknowledged his debt to the accumulated wisdom of mankind; the books he read so eagerly had helped him to rediscover the truths hidden from most men. Preparing for the trials that he knew were in store for him, Gandhi disciplined his body and his spirit, renouncing all desire for material wealth and reducing his life to one of deliberate simplicity and poverty.

By the time Gandhi left South Africa for India he had given up the practice of law for the practice of politics. His theories on the governing of men were in direct contradiction to those of Machiavelli, the influential Italian statesman, who declared that power is the common denominator of politics and that any means is justified in obtaining an end deemed to be good. Gandhi insisted that morality must be part of the science and practice of government. If the goal is good, the means of obtaining the goal must also be good, he said, else the goal will be corrupted. "Impractical," "visionary," "doomed to failure," said his detractors. "Natural," "effective," and "ultimately victorious," Gandhi replied.

Calm and confident, the little brown-skinned man voyaged toward India, his homeland, toward his most formidable opponent, the mighty British Empire. Before long the white masters of India would be confronted by an aroused nation led by a puny little man bearing an "all-sided sword."

9

Amritsar

"Last night," said Gandhi to his friend Chakravarty Rajago-palachari, "the idea came to me in a dream that we should call on the country to observe a general hartal." A hartal! — a general strike! India's politicians breathed a sigh of relief. At last Gandhi had come to his senses. At last he had seen that India must act against British rule. But what a dramatic plan he proposed! Could India carry it off?

Four years had passed since Gandhi returned to his homeland in 1915 and until now he had been a disappointment to India's politicians. They had expected strong leadership from the hero of the successful Satyagraha campaign in South Africa but, during his first years back in India, Gandhi had tried to still the clamor for action. He had said that India was not yet ready for a Satyagraha campaign against the British raj (rule). "Perhaps," India's leaders had thought, "this little man in the flapping turban is not as great as we thought him to be. He must see how India suffers, yet he holds up his hand and says 'Wait.'"

India was poor — desperately poor — under the British raj. Seeing their country's once-thriving export trade with Britain choked off by harsh tariffs, her raw materials exploited by her white masters, her people heavily taxed, India's leaders laughed bitterly when the British assured the world that they had brought the benefits of Western civilization to a backward country. Profit for Britain, not the welfare of the people, was the Englishman's guiding principle in India. From that source had sprung a host of inequities and humiliations.

Britain's immensely profitable position was bought by power and maintained by a constant display of power. Officially, the white "sahibs" reminded the Indian people of England's might by dazzling military parades and impressive ceremonies. Socially, they upheld the white supremacy principle by remaining completely aloof from the people they ruled. They moved in a world bounded by their offices, their comfortable homes and their clubs. They saw the Indian people, for the most part, simply as turbaned, salaaming servants who swept and scrubbed, who tended one's children and drew one's bath. These people were no problem to the British — they knew their place and stayed in it — it was the others, the educated Indians, who needed careful handling. To these the English offered chilly good manners. There was no point in trying to get to know these people; they would only become confused and forget that no matter how educated they were they were still Indians and, therefore, inferiors. It was, of course, expensive for the British to live as luxuriously as they did, but that was not a matter for concern — their brown-skinned subjects' taxes paid the bill.

Discontent was inevitable and by the time Gandhi returned to India voices of dissent were ringing out loud in the Indian National Congress. England had encouraged the formation of the Congress, seeing it as a relatively harmless outlet for grievances and recommendations for reform. So it proved to be. There were endless Congress debates between those who leaned toward appeals to the British for relief from repressive laws and those who advocated terrorist activity as a way of regaining national dignity, and all the debates came to nothing: the terrorists could not amass enough power to overthrow the British; the advocates of re-

Mahatma Gandhi, leader of India, photographed at his spinning

Typical crowd of followers who have come to attend one of
Gandhi's prayer meetings. This one is at New Delhi.

Gandhi's wife Kasturbai in 1939.

form were too weak to press their demands. Frustrated,
Congress leaders turned to Gandhi for guidance but his
advice seemed foolish to them. He told them that India
should first cure her own evils before considering those of
the British raj. Laziness, defeatism, drug addiction — these,
he said, were the first opponents of the Indian people to be
conquered. Besides, he added, patience with the English
was indicated — Britain had spoken of Dominion Status for
India.

At the outbreak of World War I Congress leaders had seen
a chance to exert real pressure on Britain. India will cooperate with the Allied war effort, they said, in return for
self-rule. Britain replied with a vague statement implying
that at the end of the war changes would be made leading
toward "responsible government in India as an integral part
of the British Empire."

Gandhi pinned his hopes on this hint of Dominion Status.
He liked the English people he had known and he admired
the principles of the British Empire. The British were not
evil, he said; it was their system of government in India that
was evil. As a dominion India would be an active partner
in the Empire as Canada and Australia had been for some
time and as South Africa had lately become. Congress leaders, too, were encouraged but neither they nor Gandhi were
naïve. They believed Dominion Status had been promised
them but they knew that they might have a hard time holding Britain to her promise.

It was in this atmosphere of mingled hope and suspicion
that Gandhi moved during the war years. He established
a center for community life, an "Ashram," at Sabarmati and
this Ashram, with a population varying from 30 to 230,
served as his base from that time forward. Everyone who

lived with him there had to abide by a set of rules and doc-
trines that included the taking of vows of truth, ahimsa, self-
discipline and fearlessness. Gandhi the idealist believed that
morality must be brought into politics; Gandhi the realist
knew that if the Indian people were to use nonviolence as a
weapon they must have leaders who were well drilled in its
discipline.

Seemingly unconcerned with politics, Gandhi went out
among India's downtrodden poor. He found people dumb
with despair, living in filth and ignorance. The Ashramites
must help them, he said, and Kasturbai must help too. Kasturbai was uneducated but she could teach women how to
keep their mud huts clean. Pushing aside her prejudices she
went into the untouchables' hovels and, seeing the misery
there, her heart was moved. Gently, she told an Indian
woman that she must change her dirty sari for a clean one.
"But it is the only one I have," the woman answered. Gradually Kasturbai became absorbed in her husband's mission of
service. She taught hygiene, she campaigned against the
use of drugs and liquor, and she taught peasants how to
spin their own cloth. Her two youngest sons, Ramdas and
Devadas, helped her. Harilal, still smarting under his father's refusal to give him an education, had gone into business in another city and Manilal was in South Africa, editing
the magazine *Indian Opinion.*

A year after the Allied defeat of Germany Indian hopes
for Dominion Status were rudely dashed. The Rowlatt Committee, sent by Britain to investigate the Indian situation,
recommended not more independence but rather a continuation of the wartime repressions of Indian civil liberties.
When the Committee's recommendations passed into law,
Indians everywhere demanded action. It was then that

Gandhi had his "dream" of a hartal, and emerging from political obscurity, he called for a nationwide twenty-four-hour strike as a prelude to a general satyagraha campaign against British repression.

The hartal was a spectacular success. Throughout the length and breadth of the country all activity stopped; villages and cities were silent; it was as though all India were holding its breath. The British looked on and worried. The Indian people, sensing the power that lay in their great numbers, looked up from the dust and felt a new pride.

But all did not go as planned; riots and shootings erupted in the city of Delhi and in the central province of the Punjab. Gandhi, rushing to the scene of the disturbances, was stopped by the police, escorted back to Bombay and then released, but false rumors of his arrest touched off new riots in Bombay and Ahmedabad. Gandhi was appalled. He saw the whole idea of peaceful protest being lost in the scuffle of flailing fists and flashing knives. He announced that he had made a "Himalayan miscalculation" and dramatically called off the whole satyagraha campaign. There was no point in continuing the protest, he explained, until the people were better schooled in the practice of nonviolence.

But violence could not be so easily quelled. In the Punjab a dark night of blood and terror descended on the city of Amritsar. The British authorities there, frightened by the rioting and humiliated by the successful hartal held by the people of the city, made a show of strength by deporting two local Congress leaders. The British had blundered badly: these two men, a Hindu and a Moslem, were the only ones influential enough to hold the people in check.

Leaderless and unrestrained, mobs stormed through the streets of the city, demonstrating against the deportations.

Three Englishmen were brutally murdered and several others were assaulted. Retaliating, the British issued a proclamation on April 12th prohibiting all public meetings in the city. The next morning the proclamation was read out in public to groups of Indians in various parts of the city, but later investigations revealed that many people in other parts of Amritsar were unaware of the order. That same afternoon a large unarmed crowd assembled in Jallianwalla Bagh, a vacant lot used frequently for fairs and public gatherings. Though the word *Bagh* means "garden," the area was in reality just a large debris-littered space surrounded on all four sides by the rear walls of houses several stories high. At either end of the lot there were narrow spaces through which people could pass in and out and, at one point, for about a hundred feet, the area was bounded not by a building but by a wall about five feet high.

While the assembled Indians listened to a speaker, Brigadier General Reginald Edward Harry Dyer, posted to Amritsar just two days earlier, approached the Bagh with fifty soldiers armed with rifles, forty soldiers armed with knives, and two armored cars. Unable to get his armored cars through the narrow entrance, he entered the area with his foot soldiers, stationed twenty-five soldiers on each side of the entrance and, without any warning to the crowd, ordered his men to fire. The firing continued steadily for ten minutes while the crowd tried desperately to escape. Few were able to make it to the narrow exit at the other end of the Bagh and thousands attempted to scramble over the five-foot wall. When the rifles were finally silenced, 379 people lay dead and 1137 were wounded. The biggest heaps of the dead and wounded lay on either side of the low wall. Dyer made no attempt to give medical aid to the wounded and, as darkness fell, the British-imposed curfew forced the horror-struck

Indian people of the city to abandon their own efforts to help the wounded and remove the dead.

The shock of the blood bath in the Bagh reverberated throughout all of India. The British appointed a commission to investigate the events in Amritsar and, on the completion of the investigation, published the results. Dyer's testimony before the commission revealed that he was blandly certain that he had done "the right thing." He admitted that he had directed his soldiers' fire to the points where the crowd was the densest and when he was asked if he would have opened fire with machine guns had the passage been wide enough to accommodate the armored cars, he answered, "I think, probably, yes." The British government issued a statement officially regretting General Dyer's brutality but, to the Indian people, the massacre at Jallianwalla Bagh remained a tragic symbol of the "white master" principle.

Before Dyer was called to account for his actions he was able to add excruciating humiliation to the critical injury he had already inflicted on the people of Amritsar. Three days before the massacre at the Bagh, an Englishwoman had been assaulted by an Indian mob and, several days after the events at the Bagh, Dyer announced that any Indian who wished to pass along the street where she had been attacked, would have to crawl on his hands and knees. In addition, Dyer ordered that in certain areas of Amritsar all Indians would have to alight from vehicles and salaam whenever they passed a British officer.

Jallianwalla Bagh and Dyer's "crawling order" shocked millions of Indians into wholehearted commitment to the Satyagraha struggle. The images of the dead and wounded in the Bagh and of Indians crawling on all fours before their British masters were deeply etched in Gandhi's heart. Charles F. Andrews, one of Gandhi's closest friends, wrote,

"No one can understand . . . Gandhi's attitude towards Great Britain and the British Empire unless he has come to realize that 'Amritsar' was the critical event which changed Gandhi from a whole-hearted supporter into a pronounced opponent."

10

Noncooperation

IN 1920 GANDHI proposed to the Indian people a campaign of deliberate noncooperation. The British, he said, could not continue to rule India indefinitely without the people's collaboration in their own subjugation; British power faced with steadfast noncooperation would inevitably wither and fail.

Gandhi told his people that when they wore European-style clothing made of English cloth they were imitating their conquerors and, at the same time, enhancing British wealth. By sending their children to English-run schools to be educated from the English point of view, Indians were forging more chains to bind their motherland. In accepting English honors and titles, Indians paid tribute to the principle of English superiority. The use of the English language by Indians only reinforced the walls of the prison that enclosed them. We have been slaves, Gandhi told his people, let us stop cooperating in our own slavery!

Noncooperation! The word seemed to be a magic wand waved over a sleeping land, awakening a consciousness of national pride, melting away the burden of fear that had cast the people's eyes down to the dust. Throw off your shame, Gandhi called out to India, you are no longer weak; you are armed with a weapon before which even the mighty must bow. All over India men and women heard his voice and straightened up, their hearts filled with hope.

The Congress adopted Gandhi's noncooperation program and thousands of India's patriots flocked to join its ranks. Jawaharlal Nehru, a young English-educated lawyer, threw himself into politics, intoxicated by the new sense of pride that Gandhi was giving India. In his autobiography, *Toward Freedom,* he wrote of those days:

> We said what we felt and shouted it from the house-
> tops. What did we care for the consequences? Prison?
> We looked forward to it; that would only help our
> cause still further.

Thousands of students left the English schools to continue their studies in the new Indian schools financed by contributions pouring in from every corner of the country. Native languages began to replace English. Lawyers, refusing to practice in British courts, gave up their professions and looked around for other ways of earning their livings. Rabindranath Tagore, India's poet laureate and Nobel Prize winner, proudly renounced his British knighthood. The peasants "noncooperated" by refusing to pay taxes or buy the liquors from which the government had derived enormous revenues.

Now Gandhi who, as a law student, had tried to look like an English gentleman and, as the leader of South Africa's Indians, had insisted that his wife and children dress in a "civilized" fashion, made a drastic change in his own way of dressing. Wanting to identify himself with the lowliest of India's poverty-stricken masses he abandoned the Indian-style shirt and trousers that he had worn since his return to India and commonly appeared in nothing more than a loincloth. He traveled all over India (third-class, in order to get closer to the people) addressing huge mass meetings of Indian peasants and begging them to engage in a vast campaign of self-improvement. There would be no room in the new India, he said, for the factional strife that often divided the Moslems and the Hindus; he told the people that if they wanted *swaraj,* or self-rule, they must rid India of the evil heritage of untouchability.

Gandhi urged the Indian peasants to revive their neglected village industries and, by learning how to spin and weave cloth, to stop up the drain of India's wealth to Britain's textile industries. The little bare-legged and bare-chested man was so persuasive that many an Indian peasant literally gave the shirt off his back for the cause of swaraj and then added his jacket and his trousers too. To dramatize the boycott of foreign cloth Gandhi made collections at his mass meetings of the foreign-made articles of clothing that the peasants were wearing at the time, and when a huge pile was assembled it was set afire. Crowds of peasants ringed the bonfires, clapping and shouting *"Gandhi ki jai"* (Victory to Gandhi) as they saw the hated British raj symbolically consumed in the flames of their own clothing. Materially, the Indians had, almost literally, nothing and after Gandhi passed through their villages they had even less, but in a spiritual sense, he enriched them bountifully: all over the country self-defeating lethargy was replaced by a desire to work and to work hard, hope vanquished despair and the new and exhilarating sense of pride took the place of shame.

Back in England the government authorities were seriously disturbed by the Indian noncooperation movement. Not only was there a distressing current of discontent running through the whole of Britain's largest and most lucrative colony, but this discontent was having a most unfortunate effect on the British economy. By 1921 the Gandhi-inspired boycott of foreign cloth had closed down many English textile factories and whole sections of the British population had, as a result, been thrown out of work. And it was a particularly difficult situation to deal with. A bona fide mutiny could in good conscience be ruthlessly put down by force, but the British government recognized that even the most elastic imagination would have difficulty in seeing peaceful noncooperation as mutiny.

In their perplexity the British decided to apply their age-old formula for soothing restless colonial subjects — a royal visit. A member of the Royal Family would be sent to India to demonstrate the Crown's concern for its brown-skinned subjects and to treat them to a proud show of pomp and splendor. The British did not overlook the fact that the magnificence of a royal entourage inevitably carried with it a potent reminder of the strength that lay behind it. In the case of India, the native princes, who retained their fabulous wealth and power in return for cooperation with the British, could be counted on to enhance the glitter of the show.

The logical candidate for the royal job was Edward, the twenty-seven-year-old Prince of Wales, a debonair young man whose charm and good looks and well-publicized escapades had endeared him to the Empire. Toward the end of 1921 it was officially announced that the Prince of Wales would shortly make a tour of India. The Indian National Congress reacted to the announcement by calling for a nationwide boycott of the royal visit.

When the Prince's ship landed at Bombay, seven bejeweled and colorfully costumed maharajahs and nawabs and a large contingent of handsomely uniformed government officials were on hand to welcome him, but the Indian populace was conspicuous by its absence. When the Prince rode through the streets of Bombay a group of natives who had ignored the Congress call for a boycott and had come out to see the princely show, was promptly set upon by an angry mob and a bloody riot was the result. That night the Prince with macabre aplomb cabled his father, the King: "Arrived safely. Fine trip. Only 400 killed and wounded."

In spite of its inauspicious start the tour set out from Bombay as planned on what was to be a four-month, 11,000-mile trip through the cities of India. The Prince's retinue, including the maharajahs and the nawabs and a small army of servants, numbered 100. The royal party traveled in two private railroad trains while a third carried a string of polo ponies lent to the Prince by the Indian potentates for the duration of his visit.

In each city the Prince, smartly gotten up in military uniform and pith helmet, rode through the streets in a horse-drawn carriage under a huge gold-embroidered umbrella. Behind and ahead of the royal carriage Indian and British soldiers in full-dress uniform rode on high-stepping horses, their steel lances glittering in the sunlight. Military bands blared out rousing music, flags and banners fluttered in the hot breeze and lavishly bedecked elephants lent their ponderous dignity to the rear of the procession. But all the pomp and ceremony that the British authorities were able to muster could not hide from the young Prince the fact that the crowds of loyal enthusiastic subjects he had expected were nowhere to be seen. Hartals followed him everywhere he went and he passed through deserted streets or saw Indian men and women turn their backs as he approached.

Everything that could be done to counter the Congress-ordered boycott was done even at the risk of offending the Prince. Recalling his chagrin at seeing trucks circulating through the streets bearing signs that read "COME AND SEE THE PRINCE AND HAVE A FREE RIDE," Edward noted in his memoirs that this was "a form of enticement that never had to be employed when my father travelled around India." "Gandhi's ominous shadow," he wrote, "fell often across my path and especially in the native sections of the swarming cities the struggle for the loyalties of the masses seemed to me to be a bidding match between the Government of India on the one hand and Gandhi on the other."

English officialdom did its best to distract the Prince's attention from the distressing lack of Indian enthusiasm for his visit. At the end of each day he was feted at a garden party and this was followed by a formal state dinner. Ample time was set aside on weekends for royal participation in polo matches and the Indian princes vied with each other in providing exotic forms of diversion and sumptuous displays of wealth. The Maharajah of Mysore had his bearers put on an exhibition of the trapping and training of wild elephants and then beat the Prince at squash racquets. The Maharajah Scindia of Gwalior proudly exhibited his two children, dressed in khaki uniforms, whom he had judiciously named "George" and "Mary" after the Prince's parents, and a Sikh maharajah in Patiala showed off his fleet of ten Rolls-Royce cars. In Kashmir devil dances ended an evening of lavish entertainment and the Prince rode off to bed on an elephant.

The evenings and weekends were a delight to the pleasure-loving young Prince, but his weekday duties filled him with gloom. It was particularly bad in Allahabad, Jawaharlal Nehru's home town. A few days before the Prince was scheduled to arrive there the authorities made wholesale arrests of Allahabad Congress leaders in the hopes of disorganizing their carefully planned boycott, but the arrests seemed to stiffen rather than break the people's will. Emerging from the train at the Allahabad station and riding through the native sections of the city, Edward saw only closed bazaars and shuttered windows and an ominous silence filled the troop-lined streets. "It was a spooky experience," the Prince wrote later. "I attempted to maintain a rigid and majestic pose in the carriage in order to show that I had risen above the insult."

But the insult rankled. "Dearest Papa," Edward wrote to

the King. "Well, I must at once tell you that I'm very depressed about my work in British India as I don't feel that
I'm doing a scrap of good; in fact I can say that I know I am
not." The King hastened to reassure his son by return mail:
"I quite understand that you are depressed and discouraged
by what you have seen, in the way that the natives have
boycotted you in different places where they have been
intimidated by Gandhi. But I assure you in spite of it all,
you have done and are doing good work for the Empire &
your visit is really giving pleasure to the natives although
they are not allowed to show it." Gandhi, himself, tried to encourage the young man; he issued a public statement deplor-
ing the violence at Bombay and assuring the Prince that the
Indian people held nothing against him personally — that it
was the British raj they were protesting.

While the disheartened heir to the British throne rode
through the empty streets in his sumptuous carriage, his
impoverished subjects, peeking at him from behind their
shuttered doors and windows, were elated. Many of their
friends and neighbors had been arrested for helping to organize the boycott, but that didn't matter — in fact, the more
arrests the authorities made, the better everyone seemed to
like it. Going to jail for "the cause" had become a wildly
popular fad. The Prince's visit to Allahabad had been the
occasion for Jawaharlal Nehru's long-anticipated first arrest,
and once in jail, it seemed to him that everybody wanted to
join him:

> Young men and boys would crowd inside the police
> trucks and refuse to come out. Every evening we could
> hear from inside the jail, truck after truck arriving out-
> side heralded by our slogans and shouts. The jails were
> crowded and the jail officials were at their wits' ends

at this extraordinary phenomenon. It happened sometimes that a police truck would bring, according to the
warrant accompanying it, a certain number of prisoners . . . Actually, a larger number than mentioned
would emerge from the truck and the jail officials did
not know how to meet this novel situation. There was
nothing in the Jail Manual about it.

Even the children felt the exhilaration of sacrificing for
their country's future. The jail-going campaign broke up
hundreds of families and Indian boys and girls cheerfully
moved to the homes of aunts and uncles and grandparents
until their parents could claim them. In her book *Prison and
Chocolate Cake,* Nehru's niece, Nayantara Pandit Sahgal,
told what noncooperation meant to her and her sisters, Lekha
and Rita:

> Our earliest association with politics was far from
> unpleasant. One day, when I was about three years
> old, we had chocolate cake for tea. It was a treat be-
> cause ordinarily we had bread and butter. It was a
> rich, dark cake, chocolate through and through, with
> chocolate swirls on top. While we were at tea, a group
> of policemen arrived at the house. When Lekha
> asked why they had come, Mummie explained that
> they had come to take Papu [her father] to prison, but
> that it was nothing to worry about, that he wanted to
> go. So we kissed him goodbye and watched him
> leave, talking cheerfully to the policemen. We ate our
> chocolate cake and in our infant minds prison became
> in some mysterious way associated with chocolate cake.
> It was an apt introduction to Gandhiji's teachings,
> for according to him prison should have no unpleasant
> associations. Arrest was to be voluntarily courted and
> imprisonment gladly accepted. It was not an evil to

be reluctantly borne. As we grew older, we saw that
jail-going was always treated as a gala occasion, not a
somber one. It was accompanied by a great deal of
laughter and congratulations and mutual back-slap-
ping. It made friends of total strangers, Spartans of
soft-living comfort-lovers . . . Seeing Mummie, Papu
and all the family go to jail, we longed to be old
enough to go too.

Thousands of Indians were in jail but, strangely, Gandhi
was still at liberty. He was busy leading the noncooperation
campaign, issuing directives and encouragement, constantly
warning against violence or a spirit of hatred. Every important leader of the protest movement except Gandhi was in
jail. Why was he still free? The British were mortally afraid
of the little man in the loincloth. If they arrested him there
was a real possibility that the Indian army and police would
revolt.

Pressing his advantage, Gandhi announced that an experiment in civil disobedience would be held in the county of
Bardoli, near Bombay, but, suddenly, just before the scheduled starting date for the disobedience campaign, Gandhi
cancelled it. In Chauri Chaura, eight hundred miles away
from Bardoli, villagers, enraged by police interference with
a legal procession, had set fire to a police station and then
brutally murdered twenty-two policemen. To the disappointment and despair of many of his ardent supporters,
Gandhi considered this isolated case of Indian violence suf-
ficient reason to call off the Bardoli campaign and postpone
all plans for mass civil resistance. Until further notice, only
individual noncooperation would be encouraged.

Nehru and other Congress workers languishing in prison
were understandably angry. It seemed to them that the

dangers they had faced and their cheerful acceptance of the hardships of prison life had been in vain. How could Gandhi hope to succeed, they asked, when he allowed an eruption of violence in a remote village to interrupt the whole carefully planned and sacrifice-laden Satyagraha campaign? Many Indian hopes were dashed and the British star, seemingly on the wane, began to rise again.

But Gandhi remained India's leader. Though he was doubted and criticized by many of his associates, they stayed at his side. The mass of India's peasantry was puzzled and, for a time, demoralized by the sudden suspension of plans for civil resistance, but when Gandhi called to them again they answered. What was Gandhi's magic? Did it lie within himself or within his revolutionary method?

11

Saint or Politician?

GANDHI, HIMSELF, gave a penetrating clue to his enormous hold on the Indian people. "Men say I am a saint losing myself in politics," he said. "The fact is that I am a politician trying my hardest to be a saint."

It was Gandhi the politician who appealed most to the realists among India's intellectuals and educated middle class. They remembered the astonishing success of nonviolent resistance in South Africa. They saw that under Gandhi's influence fear and apathy melted away and the Indian people woke up and set to work. They noted that, like successful politicians everywhere, Gandhi was an enthusiastic and effective fund-raiser. From the wealthy he extracted huge sums of money for the cause and from the middle classes he cajoled their gold earrings, bangles and bracelets, cheerfully assuring them that these adornments stood in the way of their becoming good Satyagrahis. India's realists — men like Jawaharlal Nehru — looking for a leader "who would win," were impressed with Gandhi's uncanny knowledge of just when the Indian people were ripe for action; for these men nonviolence was not a philosophy of life but the only effective weapon open to a weak people in a contest with a mighty opponent.

India's idealists saw Gandhi as a saint — a fearless leader who, wanting nothing for himself, was single-mindedly determined to bring out the best in India. His technique of nonviolence, demanding love and consideration for the opponent, was morally above reproach and it was clear that

Gandhi, calling out to India's soul, practiced in his own life everything that he preached.

He had an almost supernatural bond with the Indian peasants. When he addressed their mass meetings an electric current seemed to pass between the little brown man and his audience. It didn't matter that only those closest to him could hear what he was saying; men and women at the back of the crowd who could barely see him wept with joy at being in his presence. It seemed to them that he had been divinely appointed to lead them out of their darkness and into the light. They sensed that he understood their poverty, their ignorance and their misery. He spoke directly to their hearts and, in the slight figure dressed only in a loincloth, the Indian peasants saw all their own yearnings for freedom and dignity.

The masses of India's poor called Gandhi "Mahatma" (Great Soul) though he protested vehemently against the title and grew angry when they ascribed godlike powers to him. "Blind adoration, in the age of action," he said, "is often embarrassing and equally often painful." He insisted that he was only an ordinary man trying to be good and he seized every opportunity to puncture what he considered to be an inflated estimate of him. When an old peasant wearing a picture of Gandhi around his neck approached him and, weeping for joy, announced that the Mahatma had cured him of paralysis, Gandhi retorted, "You will oblige me by taking that photograph off your neck. It is not I but God who made you whole." Another time, when villagers told him that after his visit their well, which had gone dry, gave water again, Gandhi said, "You are fools. Beyond doubt it was a coincidence. I have no more influence with God than you have." Nevertheless, wherever he went people pressed around him trying to get close enough to kiss his hand or the edge of his shawl, and millions of Indians believed that they received a *darshan,* or blessing, by just catching a glimpse of him. Gandhi continued to object, but the people continued stubbornly to adore him, and his English friend C. F. Andrews said that he "groaned under the weary weight of his Mahatmaship."

His personal charm was overwhelming — almost everyone fell under its spell. He was homely and he was humble, but he had the power to move men's souls. The impression he gave of unyielding strength and deep involvement in humanity completely overshadowed his unimpressive appearance. Frazier Hunt, an American reporting on an interview with Gandhi, recalled that he had "eyes that were deep with pity and love and burning bright with a great purpose. You forgot that he was a frail little man with a funny shaven head and hollow shallow cheeks with most of his teeth gone, and that he wore coarse, homespun clothes and that his feet were bare. It was his eyes that held you." Reginald Reynolds, an Englishman who lived for a time with Gandhi at his Ashram, said, ". . . it took me a long time to understand a little about the quality in Gandhi which gave him such enormous power in India . . . While I was with him I liked, respected and admired him — but I searched in vain for some invisible quality in him that made him the lodestone of men's hearts and souls. It was not until I left him that I found he had added my own to his collection."

To Gandhi's closest friends and associates he was "Bapu," an affectionate term meaning "father," or "Gandhiji," the "-ji" suffix implying respect. Their regard for him remained constant and they addressed him as Bapu even when they disagreed with him or questioned his methods.

Outspoken criticism of Gandhi was common among the

ranks of the higher echelon of his advisers and co-workers. Jawaharlal Nehru had become Gandhi's intimate friend as well as his political disciple, but he was never his yes-man. He made no secret of his distaste for some aspects of Gandhi's policy. He didn't like either the religious emphasis in Gandhi's politics or his conviction that village industries and the moral purification of individuals were the main keys to India's salvation. Nehru had set his sights on a vast change in India's social system and he felt that Gandhi's outlook was "narrowly moralistic" and "unscientific."

Gandhi encouraged dissent and gave each of his critics a careful hearing. In many cases he went further and published their criticisms in his newspaper, *Young India*. Sometimes he modified his line of attack but always he insisted on being answerable only to his own conscience. He recognized that nonviolence could become another form of violence and he worked feverishly to maintain control of a movement that had awakened India to a sense of its own power. The violence in Bombay and the murders at Chauri Chaura finally convinced him that the people must have more spiritual training before they could keep their passions under control. "We dare not enter the Kingdom of Liberty with mere lip service to Truth and Nonviolence," he said. "Suspension of mass Civil Disobedience and subsidence of excitement are necessary for further progress . . . In order to be fit to save others we must try to save ourselves."

And so, to the relief of some of Gandhi's friends and to the annoyance and despair of others, mass civil resistance was postponed. The fever pitch of excitement gradually died down and life began to return to pre-Gandhi normality. The relaxation of tensions convinced the British that they could safely punish the source of all their troubles and they arrested Gandhi. The charge was sedition and it was based on three articles which had appeared under his name in *Young India* at the end of 1921 and the beginning of 1922. There were few who would quarrel with the contention that these articles had been designed to incite rebellion against British rule. "We are challenging the might of this Government," Gandhi had written, "because we consider its activity to be wholly evil. We want to overthrow the Government. We want to *compel* its submission to the people's will. . . . Lord Reading [the Viceroy of India] must clearly understand that the Non-cooperators are at war with the Government. . . . Bred in the atmosphere of law courts, Lord Reading finds it difficult to appreciate the peaceful resistance to authority. His Excellency will learn by the time the conflict is over that there is a higher court than courts of justice and that is the court of conscience. It supersedes all other courts."

12

Sedition — The Precious Privilege

GANDHI WAS brought to trial on March 18, 1922, in Ahmedabad. The little courtroom was packed with spectators, and British soldiers patrolled the courthouse and the surrounding area. The Mahatma had been brought before the bar of British justice and all India knew that British justice itself stood on trial.

The question of guilt was quickly decided. Gandhi was charged with "exciting or attempting to excite disaffection towards His Majesty's Government, established by law in British India." Upon being asked his plea, Gandhi replied, "I plead guilty to all charges." All that remained was to pass sentence and the judge, Justice C. N. Broomfield, said that he could do so only after hearing statements from the prosecution and the accused.

The prosecuting attorney contended that Gandhi's three articles in *Young India* were part of a deliberate campaign aimed at the overthrow of the government. He noted that though Gandhi had consistently called for a nonviolent assault, his writings had nonetheless excited the passions of the people and had led directly to the murders and destruction of property at Chauri Chaura and Bombay. It was all true, Gandhi said. He could not disassociate himself from the "mad outrages" committed by the Indian people. He had been faced with a choice between submitting to a system that was doing irreparable harm to his country and asking his people to rebel, thereby taking the risk that they would forget their creed of nonviolence. He had taken the risk and would do so again if he were set free. He was deeply sorry for the violence that had occurred and he asked for the highest penalty the law would allow. First, however, he wished to present a written statement.

Standing up before the court Gandhi read aloud a review of how, from a staunch loyalist, he had become "an uncompromising disaffectionist and noncooperator." In South Africa, despite the fact that as an Indian he had no rights, he had served the Empire loyally in the Boer War and the Zulu rebellion. At the time he had thought that the British system of government was basically good and was merely perverted in South Africa. On his return to India he had remained a loyal British subject and had placed his hopes for Indian freedom in Dominion Status. It was only when he saw that the British intended to allow the evils of the Amritsar horrors to remain uncorrected and unpunished that he could no longer find excuses for the system. It seemed to him that India was losing all her vitality under British rule and he had to act. "It has been a precious privilege for me," he said, "to be able to write what I have in the various articles tendered in evidence against me." "Noncooperation with evil," he maintained, "is as much a duty as is cooperation with good." He wished to accept the consequences of his actions and requested a stiff penalty for what he knew the law saw as a crime and what seemed to him to be his highest duty as a citizen.

The judge was caught on the horns of a dilemma. He was at once a man of conscience and the instrument of British law. In his august person English liberal tradition and ideals warred with the demands of British prestige and power. What was he to do with this bare-legged rebel who insisted on acting according to the dictates of his conscience? How should he treat this insignificant-looking man who spoke for all of India's dumb and suffering masses? The crowded courtroom hushed as Justice Broomfield addressed the prisoner:

> ... the determination of a just sentence, is perhaps as difficult a proposition as a judge in this country could have to face. . . . It will be impossible to ignore the fact that you are in a different category from any person I have ever tried or am likely to have to try. It would be impossible to ignore the fact that, in the eyes of millions of your countrymen, you are a great patriot and a great leader. Even those who differ from you in politics look upon you as a man of high ideals and of noble and even saintly life. . . . It is my duty to judge you as a man subject to the law, who by his own admission has broken the law . . .

The judge then said that he reluctantly saw it as his duty to sentence Gandhi to a six-year term in prison and added, "I should like to say in doing so that, if the course of events in India should make it possible for the Government to reduce the period and release you, no one will be better pleased than I." Gandhi replied that "so far as the whole proceedings are concerned, I must say that I could not have expected greater courtesy." It had been a most extraordinary trial. Never had there been such a bond of sympathy between a convicted criminal and his judge.

Gandhi entered prison calmly and happily, secure in his belief that in a land where a repressive government was imprisoning thousands unjustly "the true place for a just man" was in jail. Anticipating his arrest he had given careful instructions to the Indian people to remain calm and hopeful. They were to make no attempt to obtain his release; they were to continue individual noncooperation with special emphasis on the boycott of foreign cloth and the manufacture of homespun.

Less than two years after the start of his prison term

Gandhi developed acute appendicitis and was hurriedly removed to a hospital where an emergency operation was
performed. The operation was successful but Gandhi's recovery was painfully slow. The authorities thought it best
to cancel the rest of his sentence and he spent his convales-
cence at the seashore near Bombay where he received visitors who brought him up to date on developments on the
Indian political scene while he had been in prison.

The noncooperation movement had faltered and failed.
The personal sacrifices required to maintain noncooperation
at an effective pitch had been too great for the people.
Students had flocked back to the English schools and lawyers had returned to the courts. Influential Congress leaders
were favoring Indian participation in the municipal, provincial and national councils that Gandhi had asked them to
boycott. Neither discouraged nor dismayed, Gandhi decided
that he would leave politics to the Congress for a time and
in the years that followed, 1922 through 1928, he lived
quietly at his Ashram, concentrating his efforts on cam-
paigns to promote Hindu-Moslem friendship, to eradicate
untouchability and to encourage village industries. He
wrote, he lectured, he prayed and his influence grew steadily. He had not abandoned the idea of nonviolent resistance
to British rule, he had merely postponed it.

Life at the ashram at Ahmedabad was austere but, because
it revolved around the Mahatma who loved to laugh and
joke, it was far from cheerless and, indeed, a mood of good
humor and even gaiety pervaded the collection of mud-
floored huts. Gandhi took part in every activity; he conducted prayer meetings, took long walks with the Ashramites, checked on the quality and amount of their spinning
and even peeled potatoes with them in the kitchen.

And always Kasturbai hovered near him. Now, though

they no longer lived together as man and wife, a new and deeper affection bound Kasturbai and Gandhi to each other. Gandhi had given up his attempts to mold Kasturbai into his idea of a perfect wife and, strangely, she had thereupon quietly become just that. She made no demands on his time and devoted herself to her Ashram duties. Though she insisted on her prerogatives of making sure that Gandhi ate enough and didn't overwork, she stayed in the background of his life. The Mahatma belonged, she knew, not to her but to India. Gandhi called her "Ba" or Mother, and Ba she was to the whole Ashram. Her primary responsibility was the overseeing of all the Ashram's kitchens and it was generally accepted by all that it would be she who would apportion the coveted tasks of waiting on the Mahatma. Gandhi paid little attention to her, but everyone knew that he was happiest when she was nearby.

Harilal was a heart-rending problem to his parents. From the time his wife died in 1918 he had gone steadily downhill. When Gandhi frowned on the idea of his remarrying, Harilal seemed to become obsessed by a desire to hurt his father. He became a convert to Islam and it was quite evident that he had not been motivated by religious convictions, for his life had become one long, wild party. He was seen drunk and disorderly in public and he became involved in shady financial dealings. When, in one of these, he capitalized on his father's name, Gandhi publicly disclaimed any responsibility for him. He wrote a letter to a businessman whom Harilal had cheated and he printed it in *Young India:* ". . . I do not know Harilal's affairs," he wrote. "He meets me occasionally, but I never pry into his affairs . . . There is much in Harilal's life that I dislike. He knows that. But I love him in spite of his faults. The bosom of a father will take him in as soon as he seeks entrance. . . . Let the client's example be a warning against people being guided by big names in their transactions. Men may be good, not necessarily their children . . ."

Because of Harilal, Manilal, too, fell from grace. Once, when he had been entrusted with some money belonging to the Ashram, he had allowed Harilal to wheedle it away from him as a loan. Gandhi, completely unable to understand such weakness in his own son, sent Manilal away, first to an apprenticeship with a publishing house in Madras and then back to South Africa to take charge of the newspaper *Indian Opinion,* and, until the last years of Gandhi's life, Manilal was only allowed to come to India on occasional visits. Poor Kasturbai was "Mother" to a whole ashram full of people who were not related to her, and to her fell the task of raising Harilal's motherless children, but she saw her own two oldest sons only rarely and Harilal's defiance of his father had broken her heart.

Ramdas and Devadas came closest to their father's idealized concept of what his sons should be. Both took prominent parts in the Satyagraha movement and each took his turn in the jail-going campaign; both tried hard to be what Louis Fischer, Gandhi's outstanding biographer, called "junior saints."

Gandhi took the keenest delight in the children who lived at the Ashram and his own grandchildren could wind him around their little fingers. He relaxed and enjoyed them, cheerfully overlooking their shortcomings. His sons, watching him playing tenderly with their children, must have wished that Gandhi as a young father had been able to give them some of the same undemanding affection.

13

Salt

BY 1928 INDIA was seething with unrest. A British investigating commission headed by Sir John Simon had arrived with instructions to recommend reforms, but the fact that there was no Indian representation on the commission served notice to Gandhi and Congress leaders that the British were as intent as ever on playing the "white masters" of an inferior and subservient people. On its tour through Indian cities the commission was greeted with black flags and heard millions of Indian people, who knew no other English words, shouting "Go Back, Simon." A limited campaign of civil disobedience met with success in Bardoli where, six years before, Gandhi had called off a Satyagraha campaign at the eleventh hour. Police harassment in other parts of the country and new restrictions touched off widespread demands for more and bigger Bardolis, but Gandhi continued to counsel restraint and patience. It wasn't until the end of 1929 that he believed the time was ripe for an all-India civil disobedience campaign.

With Jawaharlal Nehru as its president, the Indian National Congress met in Lahore on December 31, 1929, and announced its goal to be full independence. Disappointed in its hopes for Dominion Status, India now demanded unconditional self-rule. Gandhi, it was tacitly agreed, would decide how and when satyagraha against the British raj would commence.

In an atmosphere of rising excitement the country awaited Gandhi's decision and, after more than two months of suspense, it came. "Salt suddenly became a mysterious word, a word of power," Nehru wrote. "The salt tax was to be attacked, the salt laws were to be broken." The very simplicity of Gandhi's choice of a focal issue made it dramatic and appealing. The government held a monopoly on the manufacture of salt, and British law made it a crime to possess salt that had not been made by the monopoly. The heavy tax placed on the commodity fell on rich and poor alike, but to the Indian peasant, sweating in his rice field under the hot Indian sun, salt was not a luxury but a necessity of life.

On March 2, 1930, Gandhi sent a statement of his intentions to the new Viceroy, Lord Irwin, addressing him as "Dear Friend." In his letter Gandhi explained again why India considered British rule to be flagrantly unjust and asked the Viceroy to discuss the matter with him: ". . . if you cannot see your way to deal with these evils," Gandhi wrote, "and if my letter makes no appeal to your heart, on the eleventh day of this month I shall proceed with such co-workers of the Ashram as I can take, to disregard the provisions of the Salt Laws. . . . It is, I know, open to you to frustrate my design by arresting me. I hope that there will be tens of thousands ready, in a disciplined manner, to take up the work after me. . . ." Gandhi informed the Viceroy that his aim was to move the hearts of the British people through nonviolence. "If people join me, as I expect they will," he said, "the sufferings they will undergo . . . will be enough to melt the stoniest hearts. . . ."

Lord Irwin did not answer Gandhi directly and merely sent a message through his secretary expressing his regret that Gandhi had chosen a course of action involving "violation of the law and danger to public peace." Irwin did not, or would not, understand that a deliberate "violation of the law" by normally law-abiding subjects was planned for the purpose of spotlighting the injustice of that law; he did not, or would not, recognize that in a well-disciplined civil disobedience campaign any threat to the public peace would come from the authorities themselves.

As the target date approached, all India simmered with excitement. Messages of encouragement and sympathy poured in from all over the world and foreign correspondents, together with British and Indian reporters, joined the crowds that milled around Gandhi's Ashram.

At 6:30 on the morning of March 12th, approximately 10,000 people watched as Gandhi set out at the head of a column of 79 volunteers from his Ashram on a march that was to take them to the seacoast village of Dandi, 200 miles away. There, it was announced, a breach of the British Salt Laws would be made. The sixty-one-year-old Gandhi led the march through village after village, stopping at each only long enough to ask the peasants to wear homespun, to give up intoxicating drugs and liquors, to work to eradicate untouchability and, when he gave the signal, to join him in breaking the Salt Laws.

For twenty-four days the eyes of India and the world followed Gandhi as he walked toward the sea. The government, weighing the risks it would run in arresting Gandhi against those of leaving him at liberty, did nothing. With each passing day the psychological build-up intensified. Hundreds and then thousands of people attached themselves to the procession, and men, women and children lined the route of march and tossed flowers at the Satyagrahis as they passed. Newspaper reporters flashed word of the Mahatma's progress to every corner of the country. All his countrymen's hopes and prayers were focused on Gandhi as he walked the dusty Indian roads until it seemed that he was India herself, marching toward her freedom.

On April 5th the march ended at Dandi and on the morning of the 6th, after prayers, Gandhi and the Ashramites waded into the water and then picked up some of the salt left on the shore by the sea. Gandhi made a statement to the press in which he gave the signal for all Indians to manufacture salt illegally. He urged the people to break the Salt Laws openly and to prepare themselves for nonviolent resistance to police harassment.

All over India people swarmed to the nearest seacoast to follow Gandhi's example. In *Toward Freedom* Nehru described the excitement of the time:

> . . . salt manufacture was the topic of the day, and many curious expedients were adopted to produce salt. We knew precious little about it, and so we read it up where we could and issued leaflets giving directions; we collected pots and pans and ultimately succeeded in producing some unwholesome stuff, which we waved about in triumph and often auctioned for fancy prices. It was really immaterial whether the stuff was good or bad; the main thing was to commit a breach of the obnoxious salt law . . . As we saw the abounding enthusiasm of the people and the way salt-making was spreading like a prairie fire . . . we marveled at the amazing knack of the man [Gandhi] to impress the multitude and make it act in an organized way.

Extensive preparations had been made by Gandhi and the Congress for the arrests that they knew the government would be goaded into making. Chains of command were so arranged that as each leader was arrested, another would be ready to step into his place. Volunteers, drilled in the techniques of crowd control, were charged with keeping all demonstrations nonviolent. Before long the anticipated government action began.

The authorities still considered it in their best interests to leave Gandhi at liberty and they moved first against the lesser Satyagraha leaders. Gandhi's son Devadas, his secretary, Mahadev Desai, and Jawaharlal Nehru were among the first to be sent to jail. The illegal manufacture of salt continued unabated and the police resorted to brutal methods in their attempts to seize the contraband stuff. The Indian National Congress was declared illegal and Indian newspapers, threatened with censorship, suspended publication. The people held hartals and demonstrations protesting police brutality and mass arrests were made. Soon the government jails were filled to overflowing with an estimated 60,000 offenders, but the Indian people, fearful that Gandhi might call off the protest, remained restrained and nonviolent.

Next, Gandhi notified the Viceroy that he intended to raid the Dharasana government salt works, but Irwin decided to beat him to the draw. Two Englishmen armed with pistols, accompanied by over thirty Indian policemen carrying rifles, arrived at Gandhi's camp at Dandi in the middle of the night and found him sleeping on a cot under the sky. They wakened him to inform him that he was under arrest, and while the small army waited he brushed his teeth, said his prayers and made a farewell speech to the assembled Ashramites. He then told the authorities that he was ready to accompany them and they took him by truck and special train to Yeravda Central Jail in Poona.

In spite of Gandhi's absence the projected raid on the Dharasana salt deposits took place as planned, led by Mrs. Sarojini Naidu, an outstanding Congress leader, and by

Gandhi shares a joke with Jawaharlal Nehru (left) during the All India Congress Committee meeting in Bombay, 1946. Nehru became President of the Congress later on in the session.

A typical view of Gandhi as he proceeds to a mass spinning party. He is supported by his granddaughter Tara (left) and a friend. Nehru is at the far right.

This is the kind of love Gandhi inspired. On his right is Mrs. Ava
Gandhi, on his left, his granddaughter Manu, who, not long after
this picture was taken, tried to protect him from his assassin.

Neatly arranged in the corner of a room in Birla House are all
the worldly possessions of Gandhi — a mattress, a spinning wheel,
two prayer books, an incense burner, a nickel-plated watch and
writing desk. The Burmese hat was a gift that arrived after his
death.

Gandhi's son Manilal. The foreign correspondent for the United Press, Webb Miller, accompanied the Satyagrahis and the following are excerpts from his eyewitness account of what happened:

> The salt deposits were surrounded by ditches filled with water and guarded by four hundred native Surat police in khaki shorts and brown turbans. Half a dozen British officials commanded them. The police carried *lathis* — five-foot clubs tipped with steel. . . .
>
> In complete silence the Gandhi men drew up and halted a hundred yards from the stockade. A picked column advanced from the crowd, waded the ditches, and approached the barbed-wire stockade, which the Surat police surrounded, holding their clubs at the ready. Police officials ordered the marchers to disperse under a recently imposed regulation which prohibited gatherings of more than five persons in any one place. The column silently ignored the warning and slowly walked forward. . . .
>
> Suddenly, at a word of command, scores of native police rushed upon the advancing marchers and rained blows on their heads with their steel-shod *lathis*. Not one of the marchers even raised an arm to fend off the blows. They went down like tenpins. From where I stood I heard the sickening whack of the clubs on unprotected skulls. The waiting crowd of watchers groaned and sucked in their breaths in sympathetic pain at every blow.

When the entire first column had been knocked down and carried off by stretcher-bearers a second column formed and, as their leaders pleaded with them to remember their oath of nonviolence, they marched toward the police and were methodically beaten down. Miller was sickened by the spectacle and noted that:

The western mind finds it difficult to grasp the idea of nonresistance. I felt an indefinable sense of helpless rage and loathing, almost as much against the men who were submitting unresistingly to being beaten as against the police wielding the clubs . . .

The demonstration went on for hours. Finally, when the heat reached 116 degrees in the shade, the Gandhi volunteers stopped their activities. Miller counted 320 injured; two had died. It was hard to believe that any good could come from that bloody day at Dharasana.

14

"How Can I Presume to Advise a Magician?"

GANDHI PROVED to be more of a thorn in Britain's side in jail than out. While he sat quietly in Yeravda prison, country-wide outbreaks of civil disobedience were taxing Britain's power to maintain order and filling India's jails. Demands for Gandhi's release poured into London from all over the world and English public opinion was clearly in favor of freedom for the little brown man. Bowing to overwhelming pressures, the government freed Gandhi, Nehru and other top Congress leaders.

Upon his release Gandhi requested and was granted an interview with the Viceroy, Lord Irwin. The drama of the encounter was apparent to all. In shawl and loincloth, look-ing like a parody of the humblest of the King-Emperor's subjects, Gandhi entered the splendors of the Viceregal Palace at Delhi to match wits with Irwin, tall, aristocratic, immaculately uniformed — every inch the proud representa-tive of the mighty British Empire. The two men seemed to have come to their meeting from two entirely different worlds. The real drama of the situation, however, lay in the fact that for the first time India had come not to ask a favor of England, but to negotiate on terms of equality.

The first meeting was inconclusive and others followed. Gandhi stayed at the house of a friend five miles from the Palace and often walked to his meetings with Irwin. Some-times he had his dinner — some dates and some goat milk — brought to him there and once, when Irwin invited him to tea, he made the Viceroy laugh by taking some salt from a paper bag he carried and adding it to the tea to remind

Irwin, he said, of the American Boston Tea Party. Finally, the talks culminated in a treaty, the Gandhi-Irwin Pact, an agreement that embodied a set of compromises made by both sides. Irwin agreed to release all Indian political prisoners and to permit the Indian manufacture of salt; Gandhi, in return, promised the suspension of civil disobedience and the sending of a Congress representative to the forthcoming London Round Table Conference.

The Gandhi-Irwin Pact was a striking demonstration of the power of nonviolent resistance. Seemingly, Irwin had conceded little, but much more important than the written concessions was the unwritten British admission that they could no longer hold absolute power over an India that was determined to resist them. Winston Churchill, archfoe of anyone or anything that tended to whittle away British power, thought Irwin had overreached himself and saw the pact as a deeply disturbing portent of things to come. "I am against these conversations and agreements between Lord Irwin and Gandhi," he thundered. "Gandhi stands for the expulsion of the British from India."

Some Congress leaders thought Gandhi should have held out for more British concessions before calling off civil disobedience, but the Mahatma was pleased with the compromise he had reached with Irwin and he reassured the Congress by calling the treaty a truce and announcing that the Indian goal was still complete independence. He was designated as the Congress's sole envoy to the Round Table Conference and in August, 1931, he sailed for London with a party of associates that included his son Devadas, his secretary, Mahadev Desai, and his old friend G. D. Birla, one of India's wealthiest industrialists.

Gandhi went to England to reach agreement with the British authorities on a fair constitution for India and to win

the hearts of the British people to the cause of Indian freedom. On the first count he failed, on the second he met
with gratifying success. He spent eighty-four days in England and most of this time was taken up with lectures, interviews, forums and meetings with prominent people. Churchill refused to see him but he captivated everyone else. He
made a special trip to Lancashire, a textile district hard hit
by unemployment resulting from the Indian boycott of
foreign cloth, and he was cheered by crowds of factory
workers there. Wearing sandals, a loincloth and a shawl, he
had tea with King George V and Queen Mary at Bucking-
ham Palace. When a reporter asked him if he thought he
had dressed adequately for such an august tea party, Gandhi
replied, "The King had on enough for both of us."

The British approached the Round Table Conference determined to concede nothing to Indian demands for self-rule
that would be inconsistent with the maintenance of British
power in India. Since British power and Indian freedom
were mutually exclusive, nothing was accomplished. The
bickering around the table about Hindu-Moslem differences
only served to worsen the Indian religious tensions. Gandhi,
returning to India, brought back with him nothing more
than the assurance of a huge reservoir of good will for India
in the hearts of the English people.

At home Gandhi found that the government had returned
to a policy of repression in its contest with the Indian National Congress. There had been widespread arrests and the
government had seized property and bank balances and had
suspended civil liberties. Gandhi suggested a meeting with
the new Viceroy, Lord Willingdon, but that gentleman made
it clear that the days of negotiations between the government and Gandhi were over.

Gandhi notified the authorities that he was contemplating

a new civil disobedience campaign and the Viceroy inter-
preted his message as a threat. When Gandhi denied that he
had made a threat the government ended the discussion by
arresting him under an old ordinance which made no provisions for a trial or a fixed term of imprisonment. On January 4th, 1932, Gandhi returned to Yeravda Jail.

This time Gandhi could not rest easy in jail. During his
other sentences he had relaxed and enjoyed having plenty
of time to read, believing that he was serving India just by
being in prison, but this time he felt there was more he
could do for the cause of swaraj, more he must do, even from
jail. Word had reached him that the British proposed setting
up separate elections for the untouchables, the lowest-caste
Hindus, the people whom Gandhi called the Harijans, or
the Children of God. Such separate elections would mean
that the untouchables could vote only for members of their
own caste to represent them in the legislatures and Gandhi
was determined to fight the proposal. India's Moslems and
Hindus were already politically divided by British-imposed
separate elections and if the plan for the untouchables went
through, India's unity would be still further impaired and,
worse, the gulf between the untouchables and their Hindu
coreligionists that Gandhi had worked so hard to bridge,
would be irreparably widened.

Even without British interference Gandhi's goal of integrating the untouchable caste into the rest of Hindu society
seemed almost unattainable. Untouchability was a matter
of deep-seated religious prejudice and oppression, supported
and defended by not only the oppressors, but also by those
who were oppressed. Because their religion prescribed the
rigid class system, all Hindus, including the untouchables
themselves, believed that the caste into which they were
born was not only their unchangeable fate but also their

reward or punishment for conduct in a previous life. The untouchable outcasts were sure that their only real hope for a better lot lay in living virtuous lives which would entitle them to rebirth in a higher caste. Awaiting the release of death they were resigned to their miserable existence as pariahs. They lived, unprotesting, on the outskirts of Hindu society, assigned the menial tasks of sweeping the streets, cleaning latrines and collecting garbage that were taboo for other Hindus. These lowly people were regarded as so unclean that a higher-caste Hindu, accidentally brushing against one of them on the street, hurried home to bathe and remove the stain of untouchability. They lived in squalor in city slums and on the outer edges of villages and they drank the water that collected in drainage ditches because it was commonly believed that they would pollute the village wells if they were allowed to draw their water there. Ironically, their own Hindu religion forbade them entrance to Hindu temples.

Gandhi had accepted the Hindu religion as the one that allowed him the most latitude of thought, but he blandly rejected those parts of its dogma that conflicted with his basic concept of religion. He was certain that the setting apart of any people as inherently inferior was thoroughly immoral and he saw untouchability as an immense stumbling block on the road to Indian freedom. He had worked tirelessly to bring the Harijans securely into the Hindu fold and now he saw all that he had accomplished threatened by the British move.

Oddly enough, it soon became clear that though the British had proposed the separate elections, Gandhi's fight to oppose the measure would be with his own people. It was obvious that the British sincerely believed that they were serving the best interests of the untouchables and they indicated that if the Hindus and untouchables came to an alternate agreement it would be acceptable to them. Unfortunately for Gandhi, powerful political forces on both the Hindu and untouchable sides supported the British proposal. Embittered untouchable leaders forgot the teachings of their religion and saw in separate elections a chance to get back at the Hindus who oppressed them and on the other hand, many Hindu leaders disapproved of Gandhi's crusade to bring Hindus and untouchables together and saw the British measure as an excellent means of emphasizing their separation. Undismayed by the awesome forces arrayed against him, Gandhi announced from prison that Hindus and untouchables must forget their petty differences for the greater good of all India and until they did he would fast — he would "fast unto death" if necessary. Unless the situation changed radically he would, he said, start his fast one week later, on September 20th, and once he had entered "the fiery gates," nothing could save his life but the Hindu-untouchable unity that he wanted so badly for India.

Nehru, imprisoned at the time in another jail, was shocked when he heard of Gandhi's decision. "I felt annoyed with him," he wrote in *Toward Freedom,* "for choosing a side issue for his final sacrifice." Disappointed by what he called Gandhi's "religious and sentimental approach to a political question," Nehru was tortured by doubts and worry about Gandhi's well-being. However, he finally found comfort in his faith in the extraordinary little man. "Bapu," he reflected, "had a curious knack of doing the right thing at the psychological moment."

During the week between Gandhi's announcement and the day his fast was to begin, streams of visitors arrived at Yeravda Jail and the authorities, anxious to do all they could to avoid the awful possibility of Gandhi dying on their

hands, allowed everyone free access to him. But all the con-
sultations and conferences were to no avail. On the last
day of the week there was still no agreement between the
Hindus and the untouchables. The die was cast. Gandhi
would fast.

Gandhi awoke early on the morning of the 20th and,
unable to get back to sleep, he rose and in the predawn
gloom wrote a letter to Rabindranath Tagore asking the
poet's blessing on his ordeal. He was afraid that Tagore
would disapprove of the course he was taking but he wrote,
". . . If your heart approves of the action, I want your blessing. It will sustain me . . ." The two old friends must have
been in mental communication, for later in the morning,
just after Gandhi had posted his letter, he received a tele-
gram from Tagore in which the poet said, "It is worth sacrificing precious life for the sake of India's unity and her social
integrity . . . Our sorrowing hearts will follow your sublime
penance with reverence and love."

The Mahatma had his usual breakfast of fruit and goat's
milk and then, for an hour and a half, he listened while a
companion recited the Gita to him. At 11:30 he took his
last meal — some lemon juice and a mixture of honey and
hot water. Gandhi was ready and when the jail clock struck
the noon hour the fast officially began.

During the first twenty-four hours Gandhi tried to follow
his normal jail routine and when visitors arrived to see him
he went to the prison office to receive them, but by the second day, it became obvious that he could not stand continued exertion, and the jail authorities moved him to a
secluded prison yard to which his visitors were invited to
come. There Gandhi lay on a prison mattress and sheet on
a white iron cot in the shade of a low mango tree. Near him
sat two co-prisoners, his old-time friend Vallabhbhai Patel,

and his beloved secretary, Mahadev Desai, and hovering over him was Mrs. Naidu, who had been transferred from the women's section of the prison to nurse Gandhi during his fast. On stools nearby were bottles of water and containers of the salt and bicarbonate of soda that Gandhi mixed with his water to minimize the nausea that always accompanied his fasts. Writing paper and a selection of books were close at hand. All was serene in the little yard. The Mahatma was fighting for India and, facing the physical torment of starvation, he found peace of mind.

Outside the jail political activity boiled and bubbled. Hindu and untouchable leaders met and proposed compromise measures and these were hurriedly considered, rejected, revised and reoffered. Before the first day of Gandhi's fast had passed, one proposal was found to be agreeable to all and a Hindu delegation hurried to Poona to present it to Gandhi. But Gandhi didn't like the proposition — it had too many loose ends — it wasn't foolproof. He wanted to confer with Dr. Ambedkar, the untouchable leader.

Dr. Ambedkar was sent for and he came to Gandhi's cot and assured him that he would like to help save the Mahatma's life but that he intended to sell his cooperation dearly. He made it clear that he intended to hold out for ironclad protection for untouchable rights.

By that time the fast had gone into its third day and Gandhi's condition worried his companions. The passing years had taken their toll on his ability to withstand the rigors of starvation. Heretofore, while fasting, he had always carefully conserved his strength, regularly taking salt or soda-mixed water at hourly intervals. But this time he weakened quickly and drank water only occasionally. He ached all over but waved away his friends' offers to massage his arms and legs. He had to be carried to the bathroom on a stretcher. His voice grew feeble and even the slightest exertion induced nausea. The prison doctors noted that his blood pressure had risen alarmingly. Kasturbai was sent for. She had been imprisoned at Sabarmati for civil disobedience and she was transferred to Yeravda Jail in the hopes that her presence would soothe Gandhi. As she entered his yard she tried to make him smile. "Again, the same story," she said in a mock-stern manner. It worked; he smiled; he liked having her there; if she wanted to massage him she could do so.

But soon the Mahatma was desperately weak. It appeared that his extraordinary stamina and will might have met their match in his advanced age and the debilitating aftereffects of previous fasts. And yet, amazingly, the prayers, the interviews, the conferences went on. Gandhi insisted on being pulled up to a sitting position for prayers and he would prop himself up on an elbow to whisper to his visitors.

The Indian people were in torment. Their Mahatma was fading fast. He might die and leave them. That was a possibility not to be borne. Their political leaders had failed them; they, the Indian people themselves, must save the Mahatma. The cool logic of Gandhi's previous appeals to do away with untouchability had left the Hindus unconvinced, but the Mahatma's suffering sent them hurrying to prove their love for him. Suddenly, all over India the doors of Hindu temples were thrown open to untouchables; as a demonstration of brotherly love thousands of Hindus accepted food from "unclean" untouchable hands and prominent Hindus dined publicly with the Children of God. Even the uneducated peasants were able to rise above the prejudices instilled in them by their parents and grandparents and they invited untouchables to walk on village paths and to use village wells. It was an unprecedented

phenomenon. From where he lay on a cot in a prison yard
Gandhi's intense desire for justice radiated throughout the
land and moved the hearts of millions of his people. Everywhere Hindus felt responsible for Gandhi's life or death and
they were determined that he should not die.

On the fifth day of Gandhi's fast, Hindu and untouchable
leaders, spurred on by insistent public pressure, finally
reached agreement and signed a pact that would do away
with separate elections. But Gandhi would not sign the pact
nor would he break his fast yet. The British had said that
they would accept such a Hindu-untouchable agreement,
but he must have their definite ratification of the pact before
he could sign it. He would fast until he heard from the
British.

Early Monday morning, September 26th, news came that
the British had approved the pact. Gandhi was overjoyed,
but he could not yet eat — he must first see the text of the
British approval — he was afraid of hidden loopholes. While
he waited for the text to arrive Gandhi received a visit from
Tagore. The poet, seeing the Mahatma weak and in pain,
was so overcome with emotion that he put his head on
Gandhi's chest and wept. He recovered himself, however,
and sat at Gandhi's side, talking quietly to him. Gandhi, too
weak for conversation, nodded and smiled.

Finally, it was over. The text of the British approval arrived, Gandhi pored over it and found no fault. India's
torment was over. The Mahatma would take food and live.
Quickly, preparations were made for the formal breaking
of the fast. Water was sprinkled on the dirt floor of the
yard to keep the dust down and the Ashramites, who had
hurried to the jail when they heard of the pact, assembled
around Gandhi's cot. Tagore, Patel, Desai, Mrs. Naidu and
Kasturbai stood nearby. Hymns were sung and prayers were

said and when they were over Kasturbai handed Gandhi a glass of orange juice. As he drank, the fruits and sweets that had poured into the jail as tokens of thanksgiving since word of the agreement had gotten out were passed around. Gandhi lay quietly on his cot and smiled. All India rejoiced. Gandhi issued a statement to the press warning Hindus that if the reforms were not continued he would not hesitate to fast again and reminding both Hindus and Moslems that strife between them would have the same result.

The Epic Fast, as it came to be known, did not end untouchability. The Indian people were not capable of immediately eliminating all traces of a custom that had been a basic part of their religion and traditions since a time before history was recorded. But an enormous change had taken place, a change that could never have come about as a result of a mere political pact. The Harijans, Gandhi's Children of God, became accepted by the other Hindu castes to a degree that few had believed possible, not because of a paper treaty but because they were beloved of Gandhi, because the Mahatma had been willing to die for them.

Gandhi was released from prison in 1933 and shortly thereafter he suspended mass civil disobedience and sanctioned only individual resistance to the continuing government repression. For the next seven years he concerned himself mainly with a campaign for the spiritual uplift of India. He lectured and wrote about the need for education, he urged the use of Indian languages and he traveled far and wide encouraging the development of village industries and the acceptance of the untouchables. Nehru chafed at the postponement of large-scale civil disobedience and at Gandhi's emphasis on the virtues of spinning and simplicity at a time when Nehru himself believed that India's most urgent need was for more industrialization and a greater commitment to the modern age. "Personally I dislike the praise of poverty and suffering," he said. "I do not think they are at all desirable and they ought to be abolished . . . Gandhi is always thinking in terms of salvation and sin, while most of us have society's welfare uppermost in our minds." However, Nehru had once ended an expression of his doubts to Gandhi with the words ". . . but how can I presume to advise a magician?" and the "magician" continued to win his unstinting devotion.

15

Swaraj and Partition

WHEN, IN 1939, Adolf Hitler's dive bombers shattered the peace in Europe, Britain, without consulting Indian leaders, declared India at war on the Allied side. Gandhi's sympathies openly lay with the Allies and he was filled with admiration for the gallant English people standing alone against the fury of the German war machine. He clung, however, to his belief that all violence is evil whether committed in aggression or in defense, and though he gave England his moral support, he would have nothing to do with the war effort. He went so far, indeed, as to advise the British people to abandon all but nonviolent resistance to the German onslaught. "No cause," he said, "no matter how just, can warrant the indiscriminate slaughter that is going on minute by minute." The Indian National Congress, taking a more practical point of view, announced that India would fight on the Allied side, but only as a free nation. Winston Churchill, Britain's wartime Prime Minister, laughed at the idea of nonviolence. Grimly determined to use every weapon in Britain's arsenal and pleading for more "tools to do the job" from isolationist America, he was ready to rely on his people's "blood, toil, tears and sweat" to bring Nazi Germany to its knees. The idea of Indian independence seemed equally ridiculous to him; sworn to defend the Empire at all costs, he had no intention of letting India go by default.

Britain flatly refused the Indian Congress offer of cooperation in return for freedom. When, in August of 1942, the Congress made a similar offer and authorized mass civil disobedience if it was spurned, the authorities, without waiting for the disobedience campaign to materialize, arrested Gandhi, Nehru and other prominent Indians. When Kasturbai Gandhi indicated that she would deliver the speech Gandhi had planned to make the night of his arrest, she was arrested too and imprisoned with him in the Aga Khan's palace at Poona.

Indian resentment at Gandhi's arrest set off a wave of violence that spread throughout the country. The Viceroy, Lord Linlithgow, laid the blame for the turmoil at Gandhi's door and he bridled at the charge. In a long series of letters to Linlithgow Gandhi tried to persuade him to retract the accusation and, failing, he announced that he would fast to purge himself of the unjust charge of inciting to violence. Linlithgow called the projected fast "a form of political blackmail" but Gandhi replied that it would be "an appeal to the Highest Tribunal for justice which I have failed to secure from you." Announcing that he would take only water mixed with citrus juices, Gandhi fasted for three weeks in February, 1943, and the fact that he survived seemed miraculous to most people. Winston Churchill, however, was not surprised; "It was certain," he said in his book *The Hinge of Fate*, ". . . that he was being fed with glucose whenever he drank water, and this, as well as his intense vitality and lifelong austerity, enabled this frail being to maintain his prolonged abstention from any visible form of food." Relying on his belief in the clandestine glucose feedings Churchill was sure Gandhi would live and refused the widespread demands for his release. In so doing he had taken a serious risk. After the war he wrote with renowned British understatement, "The incident was one which at the time caused me much anxiety, because Mr. Gandhi's death could have produced a profound impression throughout

India, where his saintly qualities commanded intense admiration . . ."

Kasturbai had nursed Gandhi devotedly throughout his
fast and now her own health was failing. She suffered two
heart attacks in prison and they left her weakened and depressed. Confined with Gandhi to the Aga Khan's huge,
ugly palace, she saw nothing in her surroundings to relieve
her gloom. In an effort to cheer and distract her, Gandhi
started "the lessons" again. And there they sat, the elderly
couple, heads bent over the often attempted and just as
often postponed task. As Kasturbai wrote haltingly in her
notebook and Gandhi watched and corrected her mistakes,
the thoughts of both must have flown back to the days when
a headstrong young girl had been too impatient to sit still
while her boy husband made halfhearted attempts to teach
her what he was learning in school. So many years had
passed and they had been through so much together that
it's hard to believe that either of them had much heart for
the science, geography and history that Gandhi was trying
to teach his aging wife. At seventy-three, tired and saddened, Kasturbai found it difficult to concentrate and Gandhi
was gentle with her. He must have known that in spite of
her lack of education she had, through a lifetime of sacrifice,
patience and hard work, come as close to his ideal of desirelessness as he had himself. But still they kept at the lessons.
Gandhi hoped that they would help to pass the heavy hours
and Kasturbai was still ready to do what Gandhi wanted
her to do.

In 1944 Kasturbai was stricken again. This time it was
apparent that she was dying. Unwilling to see her suffer
pain, Gandhi argued with his son Devadas against injections
of penicillin which could, at best, only prolong her life for
a day or two. Devadas allowed himself to be persuaded in

"this sweetest of all wrangles I have ever had with my father" and on February 22nd Kasturbai died quietly in Gandhi's arms. Kasturbai, who had stood by her husband through all his trials, who had suffered with him through his many fasts and had borne, unprotesting, his long struggle to make her "a perfect wife," was gone and the Mahatma was hard put to maintain his calm in the face of his cruel loss.

Six weeks later Gandhi himself was desperately ill with malaria. The Indian people demanded his release and this time the authorities, believing that he was very near death, released him and his associates. Once again, Gandhi's "intense vitality" saw him through and he was slowly restored to health.

Demands for Indian independence had, in the meantime, been mounting not only in India and in England, but also in many other parts of the world, notably in the United States. After America entered the war in 1941 President Franklin D. Roosevelt had informed Churchill of the American people's interest in immediate self-rule for India and suggested that Britain initiate a stop-gap Indian government similar to the American post-Revolutionary War Articles of Confederation. Churchill was incensed. He answered Roosevelt courteously, but in *The Hinge of Fate*, written after the war, he revealed how he felt about American meddling in British affairs:

> The concern of the Americans with the strategy of a world war was bringing them into touch with political issues on which they had strong opinions and little experience . . . In countries where there is only one race [Churchill of course overlooked the American Negroes] broad and lofty views are taken of the colour question. Similarly, states which have no over-

seas colonies or possessions are capable of rising to moods of great elevation and detachment about the affairs of those who have . . .

Impatient with what he considered to be an unrealistic, do-good attitude on Roosevelt's part, he said:

> . . . he thought of the Indian problem in terms of thirteen colonies fighting George III at the end of the eighteenth century. I, on the other hand, was responsible for preserving the peace and safety of the Indian continent, sheltering nearly a fifth of the population of the globe.

Churchill opposed Indian independence successfully for the duration of the war, but long before the Allied victory many Englishmen had, in their own minds, surrendered to the pressures for Indian freedom. Gandhi and the Indian people's Satyagraha campaign had focused English attention on the fact that the British Empire derived much of its wealth and strength from the exploitation of subject and downtrodden peoples, a fact that most Englishmen had been accustomed to rationalizing or taking for granted. There can be no doubt that the Indian people's suffering and their courageous struggle for freedom had touched and moved the collective British conscience. There are those who say that by the time Britain gave India its freedom she no longer wanted India, and in a sense, that is true. India still represented power and wealth that men like Winston Churchill were reluctant to give up, but after more than thirty years of the Indian protest, the material and, more important, the spiritual cost of maintaining the British raj had become more than the British people wanted to pay. Gandhi had never lost his love and admiration for the British people; he had faith that their high ethical standards would eventually force them to relinquish their dominion over India and, in 1945, that faith was vindicated. When the war was over events moved faster than Indian leaders had dared to hope — indeed, too fast.

Two months after Germany's surrender, Britain's Labor Party defeated the Conservatives and Churchill was succeeded by Clement Attlee as Prime Minister. After the defeat of Japan in August, 1945, the British government announced that it expected to grant self-government to India as soon as her internal problems could be solved. Every Indian rejoiced; a people who had been weak had become strong and, without violence, had wrested their freedom from their once all-powerful white masters. Britain, defeated by a peaceful revolution, was able to announce its planned withdrawal from India without bitterness and in friendship.

With swaraj in sight it seemed that the long fight was over, but Gandhi was deeply troubled — he knew that the Indian victory was only half won. The age-old conflicts between India's Moslems and Hindus had been partially submerged in the greater struggle for political freedom, but now, on the eve of independence, they loomed larger and larger until religious differences and communal tensions spread a suffocating fog over India's hopes for the future.

The mathematics of the situation were clear, but the problem of how to resolve the difficulties they presented seemed insoluble. One hundred million Moslems feared that they would be an exploited minority among three hundred million non-Moslems in a Hindu-dominated India. Gandhi had tried to convince Mohammed Ali Jinnah, the leader of India's Moslems, that religion would not be a determining factor in the government of the new nation, but Jinnah would listen to nothing that conflicted with his own plan for a Moslem state of Pakistan made up of those parts of the country where Moslems outnumbered Hindus — a state entirely separate from the rest of India. The British submitted a complex plan for a united India with safeguards for minority representation, but the Indian National Congress rejected it as too far from the India they envisaged and Jinnah would settle for nothing less than partition.

Having made the decision to grant India self-rule, Britain was anxious to get on with the job, but for more than a year the Congress and Jinnah's Moslem League could not come to an agreement about the future of the country, and until they did England could not transfer the reins of government to Indian hands. While innumerable conferences were held and propositions were offered and rejected, the bitterness of the conflict between Hindu and Moslem leaders infected the people.

Their fears inflated and their passions inflamed by Jinnah's divisive emphasis on religious differences, Moslems rioted against Hindus, who retaliated in kind. Thousands were killed and thousands more were wounded; women were abducted and men forcibly converted; temples and mosques were desecrated and property was destroyed. Gandhi, sick at heart, tried to calm and reassure the people, minimizing Moslem-Hindu differences and loudly proclaiming the greater importance of the ties that bound all Indians into a single people.

The violence overran the bounds of the cities and spilled over into the villages. Gandhi hurried to the area of the worst disturbances and wherever he went the people, in their anxiety to please him, overcame their prejudices and bitterness. Unfortunately, his soothing effect was localized and only temporary. The riots erupted anew. Gandhi, a seventy-eight-year-old man, plodded from village to village, hoping against hope to stop the whirlwind of hate that threatened to destroy all of India.

Lord Louis Mountbatten, India's last Viceroy, arrived in India in March, 1947, and plunged into lengthy conferences with Gandhi and Jinnah. Gandhi held out for a united India and Jinnah refused to consider anything but partition. Mountbatten himself was in favor of a single Indian nation, but without Moslem participation it was impossible. The poorest Moslems were willing to believe Gandhi when he told them that in a united India religious differences would be settled fairly, but the more powerful Jinnah-led middle- and upper-class Moslems had allowed their economic and religious fears to bond together in a shield that resisted even the Mahatma's pleas. Jinnah predicted civil war if Pakistan were not created and the constant riots and bloodshed seemed to bear out his prophecy.

The Indian National Congress finally parted company with Gandhi. Though the idea of partition was abhorrent to Congress leaders, in June, 1947, they reluctantly approved the creation of a state of Pakistan as the only alternative to civil war. Gandhi's plea for brotherhood, so marvelously effective in the past, had run up against a wall built of fear, greed and prejudice and, in the hour of India's greatest need, it appeared that Gandhi had failed.

16

"No Ordinary Light"

ON AUGUST 15, 1947, the work and suffering of India's long struggle for freedom were over. Britain granted independence to India and, at birth, the new nation split into two parts — India and Pakistan. Lord Mountbatten hailed Gandhi as "the architect of India's freedom through nonviolence," but Gandhi would take no part in the independence celebrations in Delhi; he was in Calcutta, in the province of Bengal, desperately trying to stem the tide of hatred that was spilling through the streets of that city.

Gandhi had never given his approval to partition, but when it was accomplished in fact he accepted it and bent all his efforts to the task of attaining Hindu-Moslem friendship. He was certain that until the Indian people could live together in peace their hard-won swaraj would be no more than a mockery. When his pleas for reason and tolerance failed, Gandhi fell back on personal suffering, his most direct route of access to the hearts of the people. He fasted and the riots in Calcutta subsided. Throngs of Moslems and Hindus came to him and surrendered their guns, swords and ammunition; religious leaders pledged all their followers in the province of Bengal to peace, and Gandhi believed them and took food.

In the heart of the Indian subcontinent the bisected province of the Punjab was bearing the brunt of the tragic consequences of communal strife and partition. In the part of the province assigned to Pakistan, 7,700,000 Hindus, Sikhs and other non-Moslems, fearing the economic reprisals and the knives and torches of the Moslem majority, left their homes and set out eastward toward security in India; from the Indian portion of the Punjab, 7,750,000 Moslems fled from Hindu brutality and took to the footpaths and the bullock-cart tracks heading for Pakistan. The miseries attendant on this greatest mass migration in history were manifold. The fifteen million people on the move, fleeing death, destruction and economic ruin at home, were prey to starvation, disease and massacre en route. Moving at the speed of the bullocks pulling their carts, they progressed ten to twelve miles a day, living off the meager stores they brought with them and, when these gave out, off the land. Cholera and smallpox walked with the Indian people over the dusty plains and, as though intoxicated with hatred and death, the caravans often paused while the weary men attacked bands of refugees passing in the opposite direction. At night men, women and children huddled in doorways, in temples or in tents made of rags. The very young, the very old and the sick were carried by the able-bodied or, when their bearers could no longer keep up with the caravan, were abandoned by the roadside. Vultures hovered over the long lines of suffering humanity that stretched beyond the horizon. In the name of religion a people, newly free, had been divided and plunged into tragedy.

Gandhi was on his way to the Punjab when he stopped in Delhi, hoping to quell the riots that had broken out there. In a frenzy of vengeance, Delhi's Hindus were attacking those Moslems who remained in the city, in reprisal for atrocities committed in the Punjab. Hundreds lay dead in the streets. Making his headquarters in the home of G. D. Birla, Gandhi went through the streets of the city begging the Hindus to stop their senseless massacre of Moslems, reminding them time and again that evil cannot overcome evil. He collected money and supplies for the refugees from

the Punjab and he held prayer meetings at which he insisted
on reading portions of the Koran, the Moslem holy book,
sternly rebuking those Hindus who objected.

Gandhi's gospel of forbearance and forgiveness for Moslems marked him as a turncoat and a traitor to many Hindu
extremists. Two ultra-orthodox Hindu societies, the Mahasabha and the RSSS, were openly anti-Moslem. Aiming
at a Hindu dictatorship for India, they were bitterly opposed
to Gandhi and his talk of Hindu-Moslem brotherhood and
equality. They engaged in terrorist activities against the
Moslems and, frustrated by the Mahatma's success in calm-
ing the rioting Hindus, they saw the person of Gandhi, himself, as the greatest obstacle to the achievement of their
aims. In Poona, the center of Mahasabha activity, a group
of young men plotted to take his life.

In the face of fanatic opposition from his own co-religion-
ists, Gandhi redoubled his efforts; the major disturbances in
Delhi subsided, but scattered eruptions of Hindu violence
continued and he decided to fast. This, he warned, would
be a "fast unto death" if necessary — he would be satisfied
with nothing less than ironclad assurance of permanent
peace.

The whole world watched as Mohandas Gandhi, seventy-
eight years old, fasted to save his country from self-destruc-
tion. Lying on a cot, his legs curled under him to ease his
physical pain, the frail little man became a symbol of India's
spiritual torment. In an agony of fear lest the Mahatma die,
the people responded and quiet returned to Delhi. Bowing
to the will of their followers, the leaders of the various
religious and political factions conferred daily in an attempt
to settle their differences. On January 18th, the sixth day
of his fast, Gandhi met with delegations of all the dissident
groups, including the Mahasabha and the RSSS, and re-

ceived their assurances that from that time forward Hindus
would cease their harassment of Moslems. Weak and spent,
Gandhi was torn between his desire to live and his fear of
being misled by mere paper pledges of peace. Finally, he
allowed himself to be convinced and again signaled his
return to life with a glass of orange juice.

The day after his fast was over Gandhi heard that the
Mahasabha had already repudiated the peace pledge and
the next day a bomb exploded near the prayer meeting
where Gandhi was presiding. Gandhi pointed out that the
bomb-thrower was undoubtedly misled and deserved forgiveness.

Ten days later, on January 30, 1948, at five o'clock in the
afternoon, Gandhi was on his way to his prayer meeting.
As he walked to the prayer ground, his arms around the
shoulders of Abha and Manu, two young women relatives,
he told them that he was annoyed with himself for being
ten minutes late to the meeting. Approaching the wooden
platform on which he customarily sat, he greeted the crowd
of five hundred waiting people with the traditional Indian
salute, palms of the hands together, tips of the fingers just
under the chin. A young man stood in his path and bowed
to him. When he did not move away Manu tried to push
him aside, but he stood his ground, took a small pistol from
his pocket and fired three times. Gandhi whispered, *"Hé
Rama! Hé Rama!"* (Oh God! Oh God!) and fell.

Within a few minutes Gandhi was dead. His body was
carried to Birla House and placed on a mattress where it lay
surrounded by friends and relatives, weeping and chanting
prayers. News of the assassination raced through the city.
Nehru, hoping against hope that the report was false, hurried to Birla House and, seeing death on his beloved Bapu's
face, dropped to his knees and buried his face in Gandhi's

garments, overcome with grief. The city's people swarmed into the streets wailing and weeping uncontrollably. They surged toward Birla House, a great sea of humanity, pushing and shoving in their desire to have a last glimpse of the Mahatma.

The grieving people were permitted to file past Gandhi's body until it became apparent that the lines of waiting people were endless. The body was then taken to the roof of a terrace and placed on a tilted cot spotlighted by flood-lamps, in full view of the multitudes below. Nehru told the country of Gandhi's death in a radio broadcast. He spoke extemporaneously, his voice breaking with emotion:

> Friends and comrades, the light has gone out of our lives and there is darkness everywhere. I do not know what to tell you and how to say it. Our beloved leader, Bapu as we called him, the father of the nation, is no more. Perhaps I am wrong to say that. Nevertheless, we will not see him again as we have seen him for these many years. We will not run to him for advice and seek solace from him and that is a terrible blow not to me only but to millions and millions in this country, and it is a little difficult to soften the blow by any other advice that I or anyone else can give you.
>
> The light has gone out, I said, and yet I was wrong. For the light that shone in this country was no ordinary light. The light that has illumined this country for these many years will illumine this country for many more years and a thousand years later that light will still be seen in this country and the world will see it and it will give solace to innumerable hearts. For that light represented something more than the immediate present; it represented the living truth . . . the eternal truths, reminding us of the right path, draw-

ing us from error, taking this ancient country to freedom . . .

A madman has put an end to his life, for I can only
call him mad who did it, and yet there has been
enough poison spread in this country during the past
years and months and this poison has had effect on
people's minds. We must face this poison, we must
root out this poison and we must face all the perils
that encompass us and face them not madly or badly
but rather in the way that our beloved teacher taught
us to face them . . .

Mohandas Gandhi, the peaceable warrior, was dead —
and yet, certainly, his was "no ordinary light." Felled by
violence, Gandhi in death led his troubled people to peace;
almost overnight India's self-destroying communal strife
waned and disappeared. The assassin's bullets, taking the
breath from Gandhi's body and stilling his voice, gave new
life to his message throughout the world. Everywhere men
felt diminished by his loss and paused to consider what his life
had meant. The frail little man who left behind him nothing
of more material value than his nickel-plated pocket watch
had given his fellow men a legacy of matchless worth —
nonviolence, the "all-sided sword" that "blesses him who
uses it and him against whom it is used." His life was a
testament to his faith in the power of good over evil.

III

The American Negroes

. . . it may be through the Negroes that the unadulterated message of nonviolence will be delivered to the world.
> — *Mohandas Gandhi, 1935*

1

Mrs. Parks Refuses

IT WAS EARLY evening on Thursday, December 1, 1955, and the office buildings and department stores were spilling crowds of people onto the streets of downtown Montgomery, Alabama. Everybody was tired and everybody was in a hurry to get home. At the bus stops little knots of people hunched their shoulders against the cold as they waited. Mrs. Rosa Parks, a Negro woman, watched for the Cleveland Avenue bus and hoped that it wouldn't be crowded. She worked as a seamstress in the Montgomery Fair, one of the city's big department stores, and she'd had a hard day; it would feel very good to sit down on the way home. When the Cleveland Avenue bus wheezed to a stop in front of her, Mrs. Parks got on and thankfully sank into a seat just behind the section reserved for white people. But after a few more stops all the seats in the white section were taken and, when four more white people boarded the bus, the driver told Mrs. Parks and three other Negroes sitting near her to stand. The three other Negroes did as they were told and three of the white people took their seats. Mrs. Parks, however, stayed in her seat. Looking straight at her in the mirror above his head, the driver repeated his order, this time more firmly. But Mrs. Parks was tired and a spark of resentment had flared into rebellion. "No," she said, "I won't get up."

The white man who was waiting for Mrs. Parks's seat carefully looked the other way and the rest of the white passengers shifted uneasily in their seats. There was always an awkward moment or two when seats were given up by colored people and taken by whites. Eyes met eyes for a flashing second and unspoken words hovered ominously in the unquiet air. It was only rarely, however, that a Negro refused to obey a driver's order. There was bound to be an unpleasant scene. Everybody would be held up. Some people had no consideration for others.

In the back of the bus the Negro passengers murmured among themselves: "She must be crazy!" . . . "No, she's not crazy, she just has guts — good for her!" . . . "I'm not mixing in any trouble" . . . "He'll have her arrested" . . . "It's not going to do anybody any good anyway."

The driver put on the brake, ducked out of his seat and got off the bus. In a minute he was back with a policeman and in another minute Mrs. Parks left her seat after all — under arrest. The driver resumed his seat, shifted gears and the Cleveland Avenue bus proceeded on its way.

Mrs. Parks was taken to jail and then, when her bond was signed by E. D. Nixon, a prominent leader in the Negro community, she was released from custody and told to appear for trial the following Monday. The policeman handling her case wondered what had gotten into her on that bus. Surely this quiet, modest woman knew better than to suppose that her stubbornness could lead to anything more than a stiff fine. Mrs. Parks had no more idea than he did of what the eventual outcome of her small rebellion would be. She didn't know that a lot of other Negroes in Montgomery had also had more than they could take.

After he left the police station E. D. Nixon told some friends about Mrs. Parks's arrest, and their reaction, like his, was that something must be done about the buses. The bus company employed only white drivers and many of them were openly contemptuous of their Negro passengers.

Mrs. Rosa Parks and Mr. E. D. Nixon (left) arrive at the
Montgomery County Courthouse for her trial.

Rev. Ralph Abernathy (left foreground) conducts a mass prayer
meeting in Montgomery along with other Negro leaders who had
been indicted during the course of the bus boycott.

Rev. Martin Luther King (center) arrested for participating in the sit-in demonstrations in Atlanta in 1960.

Rev. Ralph Abernathy,
after he succeeded
King as President of the
Montgomery
Improvement Association.

Some thought nothing of calling them "niggers" and "black apes" while accepting from them the same dimes that the white people paid. Others insisted that Negroes get off their buses after paying their fares and reboard through rear doors lest they bother the white passengers on their way through to the rear section. And the policy of making colored people give their seats to white people was really too unfair. All Southern Negroes knew that the principle of "white supremacy" ruled the South and that the only way to avoid the complete segregation of the races was to pack up and go North. Segregation was something that Southern Negroes had to take but here in Montgomery the bus company had overstepped even segregation's line of decency.

A few of the women who heard Nixon's story indignantly took to their telephones and spread the word of Mrs. Parks's arrest. One of the ladies suggested that the Negroes of Montgomery show their resentment of the bus company's actions by refusing to ride the buses at all. Negroes accounted for 70 per cent of the bus company's customers, she pointed out, and their absence from the buses would surely convince the bus line's management to change its policy. The idea caught on and before long the telephone wires were humming with boycott talk. Nixon was all for going ahead with it, and the next morning he broached the subject to two men whose opinion he respected — the Reverend Ralph Abernathy and the Reverend Martin Luther King. Both men were enthusiastic.

The plan had a special appeal for Martin Luther King. He was a very young man, only twenty-seven years old, and his rather short, stocky physique was far from impressive (especially when he stood next to his burly friend Ralph Abernathy) but he had big dreams — dreams of helping the Negro people. He felt sure that a better day for Negroes lay just over the horizon and he wanted to work, and work hard, to bring that day closer. He had come to Montgomery a little more than a year before to take over the pastorate of the Dexter Avenue Baptist Church and ever since his arrival he had tried hard to awaken his church members' interest in social and political action. King's congregation had taken to their new pastor right away. He had a modest, appealing personality, but when he put on his minister's robes and stood in the pulpit he spoke with conviction and authority. His voice, rich and persuasive, reached out and touched the hearts of his listeners and his words told them that he understood what they wanted most in their lives. There was something about him that made them feel more hopeful and less afraid.

The idea of boycotting the buses was not new. Several times in the past there had been talk in Montgomery of a boycott when Negroes suffered unusual indignities on the buses, but the talk had always run up against a stone wall of Negro apathy and fears and had dwindled away to nothing. This time, however, King, Abernathy and Nixon all thought that with some organization and a lot of hard work a boycott could actually be brought into being. The Negro community was buzzing with indignation over this latest arrest and they felt that if they struck while the iron was hot this indignation could be channeled into effective action. They set up a meeting for that same night and asked all the city's Negro clergymen and civic leaders to attend. Almost everyone who was invited came and, surprisingly, everyone was enthusiastic. It would be worth a try, they all said, things had certainly gone too far. Segregation was one thing, but rank injustice was quite another. This time action, not talk, was what was needed.

How long should the boycott last? How were the Negro people of Montgomery to get to and from their work? What would be the reaction of the city's white people? Nobody at the meeting knew the answers to these questions, but in the excitement of the moment optimism conquered doubt. If there were problems, ways would be found to solve them; if there was trouble, courage would be found to face it. Something had to be done about the bus situation and a boycott seemed to be a good way of doing it.

Everybody agreed that the boycott should begin as soon as possible, while spirits were still high. The following Monday morning, the day of Mrs. Parks's trial, was set as the time to start and it was decided that a mass meeting to be held at the end of that day would determine whether or not the protest would go on. Volunteers were then enlisted to tackle the most immediate problems: notifying the city's Negroes of the boycott plans and arranging for substitute transportation.

The transportation problem was partially solved almost at once. The taxi system in Montgomery, like everything else, was black and white. Colored people took "colored" taxis; white people rode in "white" cabs. When the Negro taxi company was consulted it offered to take Negroes as passengers for the same individual fares that they would have paid on the buses. That was fine; the taxis would take care of a lot of the Negro working population; private car-pools would carry many more, and the others, perhaps, would walk.

Spreading the word of the proposed boycott among the Negro people was the next problem. The meeting drafted a notice that read:

> Don't ride the bus to work, to town, to school, or any-
> place Monday, December 5.

Another Negro woman has been arrested and put in jail because she refused to give up her bus seat.

Don't ride the buses to work, to town, to school, or anywhere on Monday. If you work, take a cab, or share a ride, or walk.

Come to a mass meeting, Monday at 7:00 P.M., at the Holt Street Baptist Church for further instructions.

The next morning 7000 of these notices were mimeographed and given to volunteers to distribute in the Negro community. Only a small percentage of the city's Negroes could be reached that way but it was hoped that word of mouth would do more of the job. But luck was one of the Negroes' volunteers that day. A colored maid was handed one of the circulars and, not knowing how to read, she asked her white employer to read it to her. Reading the circular the white lady was incensed. Thinking that the Negro people were planning something behind the white people's backs she decided that the white community should be warned. She telephoned the text of the circular to the *Montgomery Advertiser* which promptly printed it in full on the first page of their Saturday morning edition. By that afternoon every white person in Montgomery knew about the boycott plans — and so did every Negro!

On Sunday the buses were the main topic of conversation throughout the city. Most white people refused to take the proposed boycott seriously — they were sure that the Negroes had neither unity nor daring enough to make it work — but in every Negro home doubt and apprehension warred with the new and exhilarating spirit of hope. Was there really a chance of fighting the humiliation and indignity that rode in the rear section of the buses? Was the possibility of decent treatment on the buses worth taking the chance of angering the white people? In each Negro heart a decision was taken that weekend and each Negro wondered what the others would do.

Boycott! The word bothered Martin Luther King that Sunday afternoon. Ever since Friday he had been rushing to complete preparations for the bus protest and now for the first time he had a minute to sit down and think. Boycott! The word was unpleasantly tied up with the White Citizens Councils, a South-wide group of anti-Negro organizations that ruthlessly applied economic pressure on Negroes and whites alike in order to preserve white supremacy in the South. Drawing their members from the wealthiest and most "respectable" members of white communities, the WCC wielded awesome power. The Negro who forgot "his place" found that WCC pressure could force his employer to fire him; the white man who refused an invitation to join a Council found that his business was effectively boycotted. Could the Negro people, King wondered, use the boycott technique without taking on some of the evil of the Councils? If, in their fight for justice, they inflicted economic losses on the bus company might they not be using an immoral means to achieve a moral end? Sitting there in the Sunday afternoon quiet of his home King was tormented by doubts. And then, all at once, his thoughts flew back to a time when he was a student at Morehouse College in Atlanta, Georgia. In his book, *Stride Toward Freedom*, King said:

> . . . I began to think about Thoreau's *Essay on Civil Disobedience*. I remembered how, as a college student, I had been moved when I first read this work. I became convinced that what we were preparing to do in Montgomery was related to what Thoreau had expressed. We were simply saying to the white com-

munity, "We can no longer lend our cooperation to an evil system."

King told himself that the city's Negroes were not out to make the bus company suffer financially; their aim would be rather to make it clear that they could not be a party to injustice. Was it not a man's Christian duty to resist evil as well as to do good? The bus protest would be more a massive gesture of noncooperation than a boycott. Thus King was able to make peace with himself. The word "boycott," however, continued to ring harshly in his ears and in the months to follow he used it as rarely as possible.

As dusk fell on Montgomery that Sunday afternoon King's two-week-old daughter, Yolanda, opened her small mouth and wailed. It was only the natural noise that a hungry baby makes but the mournful sound sharpened the twinges of worry that were plaguing King. As his wife, Coretta, hurried to warm the baby's bottle, King switched on a lamp and went to the telephone. He would call Ralph Abernathy and see what he thought their chances of success were. The two friends talked and joked a little and tried to bolster each other's spirits, but when it came to exchanging estimates of how many of the city's Negroes would stay off the buses, King found that Abernathy was no more optimistic than he was. It would take an awful lot of very brave people to make the venture come off. Well, they wouldn't hope for too much. They would set their sights on 60 per cent. If the boycott, or noncooperation campaign, was even 60 per cent effective, they agreed, they could hope to get something accomplished.

2

"This Is Our Challenge . . ."

MONDAY MORNING, December 5, 1955. Martin and Coretta King were up and dressed at 5:30. They knew that the first bus of the South Jackson line, usually jammed with Negro maids and cooks going to their jobs, was due to pass their house at about six o'clock and they wanted to be at their front window to see it. King was in the kitchen drinking coffee when he heard Coretta cry out, "Martin, Martin, come quickly!" He ran to the living room and joined her at the window. A slowly moving bus was passing their house and the Kings could hardly believe what they saw — it was empty. Fifteen minutes later a second bus was also empty and when a third passed, it carried two white passengers riding in majestic solitude.

Joyfully, King ran out of the house and during the next hour he drove his car through all the major streets of the city, carefully checking the buses. During the peak of the morning rush hour he counted only eight Negroes on the buses. Normally, 17,500 Negroes rode the buses twice a day. Where were they? King saw them all around him — they were riding in taxis or in jam-packed private cars; some proudly rode on mules and a few had come from the outskirts of the city in horse-drawn buggies. And the others walked. The sidewalks were crowded with Negroes, old and young; domestic workers, laborers, children, college students — all cheerfully walking.

Mrs. Parks's trial was held that morning. The judge found her guilty, not of disorderly conduct as was usual in such cases, but of disobeying the city segregation ordinance. Her attorney, Fred Grey, announced that she would appeal her case to a higher court. Outside the police court, on the streets of the city, another appeal, to the conscience of Montgomery's people, was already in progress.

That afternoon an organization was formed to guide the protest. It was named the Montgomery Improvement Association, and King was elected its first president. Ralph Abernathy was appointed to draw up a set of demands that would be made to the bus company if the evening mass meeting decided that the protest should continue.

As the day wore on, the buses continued to be "white only." A new spirit was abroad among the Negro people. Strangers waved to each other; Negro taxis picked up hitchhikers and when they were full their occupants shouted encouragement to those who were walking; in colored neighborhoods children congregated at the bus stop to cheer the empty buses. It was obvious that the one-day pilot boycott had been a resounding success. Now everything hinged on the evening mass meeting. If there was a large turnout and if the people were enthusiastic the boycott could be extended; if the protest was to go on, the mood of the meeting would determine the course it would take.

Thrilled by the exciting events of the day, King was awed by the challenge they presented. Could the Negro people, he wondered, sustain a protest that would demand of them extraordinary discipline, sacrifice and patience? There was the awful possibility that, finding courage in unity, they might allow their bitterness at past injustices to spill over into violence. King was to be the principal speaker at the evening meeting and he knew that he must somehow find words that would encourage his people to press on with their search for self-respect and, at the same time, convince them of the need to conduct their protest in a spirit of love and forbearance. Again and again his thoughts turned to the Sermon on the Mount.

As King drove toward the Holt Street Baptist Church that evening he stopped worrying about whether the mass meeting would be well attended. Five blocks away from the church, traffic was jammed with cars heading toward the meeting and when King parked his car and approached the church on foot he saw that an overflow crowd of thousands of Negroes was standing outside. Pushing his way through the mass of orderly, good-humored people he felt a new confidence. He wouldn't let these people down. If they really wanted to act against injustice he would be able to help them.

The meeting was opened with a hymn, a prayer and a reading from the Bible and then King walked to the pulpit. Standing before the hushed and eager crowd he spoke of the history of abuses Montgomery Negroes had suffered on the buses. He said that the time had come to protest, ". . . to say to those who have mistreated us so long that we are tired — tired of being segregated and humiliated; tired of being kicked about by the brutal feet of oppression." Thunderous applause interrupted King and when it died down he continued: ". . . For many years we have shown amazing patience. We have sometimes given our white brothers the feeling that we liked the way we were being treated. But we come here tonight to be saved from that patience that makes us patient with anything less than freedom and justice." The crowd roared its approval.

King went on to warn his people that the value of their protest would be lost unless it was kept within the framework of Christian doctrine. "Once again," he said, "we must hear the words of Jesus echoing across the centuries; 'Love your enemies, bless them that curse you, and pray for them that despitefully use you.' If we fail to do this our protest will end up as a meaningless drama on the stage of history, and its memory will be shrouded with the ugly garments of shame. In spite of the mistreatment that we have confronted we must not become bitter, and end up by hating our white brothers . . ." As King ended his speech the crowd rose, as one man, to its feet and applause thundered to the rafters of the church.

Ralph Abernathy read out the text of the resolution he had drafted. It called on Montgomery's Negroes to refrain from riding the buses until: they received a guarantee of courteous treatment from bus drivers; passengers were seated on a first-come, first-served basis — Negroes seated from the back of the bus toward the front, whites seated from the front toward the back; some Negro drivers were employed on predominantly Negro routes. When a motion was presented it was unanimously carried by the shouting, cheering multitude.

In the Holt Street Baptist Church that night the Negro people of Montgomery woke up from their long sleep of submission. The white men might continue to oppress them but they would no longer cooperate in their own oppression. A young Negro minister had stood before them and had filled them with a new sense of self-respect. "If you will protest courageously, and yet with dignity and Christian love," he had said, "when the history books are written in future generations, the historians will have to pause and say, 'There lived a great people — a black people — who injected new meaning and dignity into the veins of civilization.' This is our challenge and our overwhelming responsibility . . ." Hearing King's words the assembled Negroes sat straighter in their seats. The burden of fear they had carried so faithfully and for so long had, all at once, grown noticeably lighter.

Later King was to deny that he had led Montgomery's Negroes to protest; he was convinced that the bus boycott would have occurred at that time and in that place if he had never been born. "I was catapulted into the leadership," he said.

Martin Luther King was right. The Montgomery protest was a people's movement and when, in the years that followed, it spread beyond that city, it remained a people's movement. It was to have many leaders, but their roles would be limited to guidance and organization of actions that sprang from the Negro people themselves. King, however, was to be the principal spokesman for the "movement." He would continue to find the words to express the yearnings of millions of Negroes and to tell their "white brothers" that they meant to push and push until they had won their freedom. What was Martin Luther King's story? How had he come to be a symbol of America's "new Negroes"?

3

King's Story

YOUNG MARTIN Luther King, Jr., hated to hear white men casually address his father as "Boy." There wasn't anything unusual about it — all white people called colored people "Boy" or "Uncle" or "Aunt" or by their first names. That was part of the normal relationship between Southern whites and Negroes and almost everybody took it for granted. But the senior King was a dignified Baptist minister, a more than usually conscientious citizen, and it just didn't seem right that he should be called "Boy" by anybody. Growing up in Atlanta, Georgia, was hard in many ways for a colored child but the way white people spoke to his father probably hurt young Martin the most.

Today Martin Luther King, Jr., is himself a minister and a father and nobody calls him "Boy." He has been asked to leave one state by its governor and warned by another governor to stay out of his. Many white Southerners refer to him as an agitator and a dangerous radical, but even his bitterest opponents concede that he is not a man to be taken lightly. King is today the outstanding leader among many leaders of America's "new Negroes," a courageous and determined group of people in peaceable revolt against the social system of segregation. His story starts with an often-repeated prayer of his father's: "Lord, grant that my children will not have to come the way I did."

King's father came a long hard way. Born on a small farm outside Atlanta, he had longed as a young boy to escape the drudgery and misery he saw all around him. Delivering clothes that his mother had washed and ironed to white families nearby, he caught glimpses of a gracious way of life that made his own seem unbearable. Plenty to eat, nice clothes, leisure to look around and enjoy living — all these the boy wanted and wanted badly. He was determined that he would have them even though his skin was black. Grasping at education as his only key to a better life, he slowly and painfully pulled himself out of the morass of poverty and debt in which his family foundered.

Because little education was available to country Negroes, he left home and went to Atlanta when he was sixteen years old and for ten years he worked days and went to school at night to get a high-school diploma. Wanting to be a minister he then went on to college. While still a student he married Alberta Williams, the daughter of a minister, and shortly thereafter became his father-in-law's assistant pastor at Atlanta's Ebenezer Baptist Church. His first son, Martin Luther King, Jr., was born in 1929.

The young Martin and his brother and sister never had to come the way their father did. They lived in a spacious, comfortable home, had nice clothes, went to school regularly and had plenty of time to play. Though the Reverend Mr. King was not wealthy, his income as a minister was far above that of the average Southern Negro and he was acutely conscious of his good fortune in being able to support his family so well. He blamed the poverty of the overwhelming majority of Negroes on the social system of segregation that had replaced slavery as an effective means of keeping colored people apart from white people, dependent and weak. He taught his children that segregation was not the natural order of things but an evil to be resisted, and he fought it as best he could by being active in the NAACP (National Association for the Advancement of Colored People) and he conducted a determined one-man boycott of the city's segregated buses.

Mr. King tried to shield his children from the humiliations of color prejudice. He limited their contacts with white people and he tried to keep them off the buses by driving them wherever they wanted to go. But, inevitably, they encountered discrimination and the heartbreak that goes with it. Suddenly, the little boy, Martin Luther King, Jr., could no longer play with the two white boys who had been his friends for as long as he could remember; their mother had decided that they had passed the age when it was proper for white and colored children to play together. Once, when the two Martin Kings, senior and junior, went downtown together to buy shoes, they were told by a white clerk in the shoe store to move from the seats they had taken in the front of the store to those reserved for Negroes in the rear. Mr. King was not one of those Negroes who could smile at such an affront and do as he was told. "We'll either buy shoes sitting here," he told the clerk, "or we won't buy shoes at all," and, taking his son by the hand, he marched out of the store.

Segregation was everywhere and no colored child could escape it. It was in the newspapers where the courtesy titles of "Mr.," "Miss," and "Mrs." were omitted in references to Negroes; it was in the movies where Negroes had to enter the theater by a "colored" door and sit in an unclean balcony; it was in the downtown lunch counters where Negroes could only be served food to "take out." In all public places there were separate washrooms and waiting rooms for Negroes and whites — even thirst was color-conscious and Negroes and whites had their own drinking fountains, often side by side. And, lest any Negro forget that segregation was serious business, the hooded and sheet-swathed Ku Klux Klan held parades and demonstrations on the city streets. Negroes who forgot their place received anonymous threats or found the Klan's symbol, a burning wooden cross, in front of their homes. Sometimes, when these warnings did not suffice, dynamite bombs were thrown at Negro homes. Though the Reverend Mr. King made no effort to hide his opposition to segregation, he was never attacked physically — a fact which his son said "filled my brother and sister and me with wonder as we grew up in this tension-packed atmosphere."

The King children went to a "colored" school. (Since 1896 Southern public school education had been based on the principle of "separate but equal," a concept which appealed to white Southerners but not to Negroes who knew that inequality was built into the separateness.) Martin, Jr., did very well in school and was able to enroll as a freshman at his father's alma mater, Morehouse College, when he was only fifteen years old.

For a long time Martin couldn't make up his mind between the ministry, the law and medicine for his choice of profession, but he finally decided that he wanted to be a minister like his father and, on graduating from Morehouse, he went as a scholarship student to Crozer Theological Seminary in Chester, Pennsylvania. Living in the North was a strange and exciting experience for King. Though Northern Negroes were by no means fully accepted in white society they enjoyed a degree of freedom that amazed and delighted the Southern boy. The segregated waiting rooms, lunch counters, buses and trolley cars that were constant humiliations to Negroes in the South were unknown in the North; most colored children went to integrated schools and the collective weight of the Negro vote was an important factor in

Northern elections. For the first time King found himself forgetting the color of his skin.

One Sunday afternoon in 1950, while he was a student at Crozer, King went to nearby Philadelphia to hear a sermon by the prominent and respected president of Howard University, Dr. Mordecai Johnson. Dr. Johnson, who had just returned from a trip to India, spoke of the life and teachings of Mohandas Gandhi, and King was so excited by what he heard that he immediately bought all the books he could find by or about Gandhi. He had always believed that Jesus' teachings of "love your enemy" and "turn the other cheek" could only be practiced in contacts between individuals, but now, in the Gandhi story, he saw them applied, and applied successfully, in a conflict between two peoples. Gandhi, he discovered, had been able to apply Thoreau's concept of civil disobedience on a mass scale, and with mounting excitement he read about the gradual but sure ascent of a downtrodden people, armed only with love and a renunciation of violence, toward justice, dignity and freedom. The social philosophies that he had been studying, those of Bentham and Mill, Rousseau and Nietzsche, Marx and Lenin, all seemed to pale beside the philosophy of nonviolence. King had become a convert to what he called "the only morally and practically sound method open to oppressed people in their struggle for freedom."

On receiving his degree from Crozer, King, top man in his class, was awarded a scholarship for two years of additional study at a graduate school of his choice and, in 1951, he drove his green Chevrolet, a graduation present from his parents, to Boston where he enrolled as a candidate for a Ph.D. degree at Boston University. He reveled in the intellectual climate of Boston and he had the added thrill of discovering the opportunities that a liberal Northern community provided for real friendships between Negroes and white people. Boston was a revelation to King in many ways but, most important of all, it provided the setting for his meeting with Coretta Scott, a beautiful young music student from Marion, Alabama, who, in 1953, became his wife.

The next year King had to make a decision that he knew would influence his whole future life. He had been offered two pulpits in the North and he had also been asked to take over the pastorate of a church in Montgomery, Alabama. Young and eager for an effective and satisfying life, King was sorely tempted by the North's comparatively liberal attitude toward Negroes. But the South was his and Coretta's home; they loved the South and they decided that they wanted to use their education to help the Negro people there.

On September 1, 1954, Martin and Coretta King moved into the parsonage of Montgomery's Dexter Avenue Baptist Church. The new minister plunged into his church duties, joined the local chapter of the NAACP and took an active part in Negro civic affairs. As he and Coretta came to know Montgomery they found that though the city was a busy center of the state's economic life, it had kept, on its tree-shaded streets and avenues, much of the charm and beauty of the old South; that somehow Montgomery had managed to merge and mingle the slow-paced grace of the past with the bustle demanded by modern business. The city had a distinctive character all its own, but the Kings soon found that in its attitude toward Negroes it mirrored and magnified that of the whole South.

Every aspect of the city's life was segregated. Transportation, civic life, religion, entertainment, business — all operated on two separate planes — black and white. Only unskilled, low-paying jobs were open to Negroes and, as a result, their standard of living was strikingly low compared to that of the white people. The white man took the privileges of adequate living space, privacy and indoor plumbing for granted; to the Negro they were luxuries that all too often he could not afford. Poor living conditions and the frustration of being cut off from all hope of changing those conditions were reflected in a high Negro crime rate; this in turn was taken by most white people, and many Negroes as well, as conclusive proof that the colored people were, in fact, inferior to the whites.

Justice was an elusive commodity for Montgomery Negroes accused of crimes. The terror and violence of the night-riding Ku Klux Klan had long been out of favor in the South, but they had been replaced by a more sophisticated injustice handed down by color-conscious all-white juries. Since its organization in 1910 for the purpose of opposing segregation and obtaining justice for Negroes in the courts, the NAACP had been helping Negroes caught in the toils of Southern law. Relying on lobbying, public education and court action the NAACP slowly but steadily attacked the legal roots of "white supremacy" and, owing largely to its efforts, Negro rights became more and more firmly established in federal law. The white South called the NAACP "agitators" and "radicals" and accused it of going too fast in its pursuit of justice for Negroes; NAACP lawyers, embroiled in the long and tedious process of court suits, wryly reflected that "if we get any more gradual we'll be backing up." King urged his congregation to be active in the NAACP and he took pride in the fact that a year after his arrival in the city, records showed that the Dexter Avenue church had led all other Montgomery churches in contributions to the organization.

Montgomery's white and colored children attended separate schools and the state of Alabama was determined that they would continue to do so in spite of the Supreme Court's ruling earlier that year that segregation in the public schools was unconstitutional. Some of the border states made plans to integrate their schools at once, but most of the white South saw the Court's decision as an unacceptable threat to the "Southern way of life" and decided on a policy of "massive resistance" to school integration. State legislatures busied themselves with creating a new body of law designed to defy or evade the Court's ruling. It seemed that the South had resolved to follow the advice of a Virginia newspaper editor who said:

> . . . Litigate? Let us pledge ourselves to litigate this thing for 50 years. If one remedial law is ruled invalid, then let us try another; and if the second is ruled invalid; then let us enact a third.

The newly formed White Citizens Councils had their own "legal" ways of opposing school integration. With one hand they wielded the powerful weapon of economic coercion and with the other they blanketed the South with literature playing on ancient fears of "mongrelization of the white race." Desegregation of the schools, the WCC warned, would be the first step toward domination of the white South by "an ignorant and revengeful black people." Fear was the lifeblood of the White Citizens Councils and, deliberately creating an atmosphere of fear and tension, they grew and flourished.

In Montgomery, as in every other part of the Deep South, white politicians tried to stifle the Negro's political voice by making it as difficult as possible for him to register to vote.

The city's citizens stood in separate "colored" and "white" lines before separate registration tables and while the white line was processed quickly and methodically, the colored line was subject to elaborate slowdowns. All would-be voters were given long and involved questionnaires to fill out and when Negro applicants did not complete theirs to the registrar's satisfaction they were kept in the dark about where they had made their mistakes. These devices were so successful in discouraging Negro voters that when Martin Luther King came to take up his duties in Montgomery, only a little more than 2000 of Montgomery County's 30,000 voting-age Negroes were registered. King set up committees in his church to instruct members in the intricacies of registration forms and to urge them to be persistent in their attempts to register and vote.

Unfortunately there was no real communication between the Negro and white peoples in the city. As a result Montgomery's white citizens took pride in the "peaceful race relations" that prevailed. They pointed out that the Negro people, while still poor, were appreciably better off than they had ever been before; that they were, on the whole, decently fed and clothed and that many of them owned cars and television sets. The white people of the city were convinced that their Negroes were "satisfied"; segregation was the Southern way of life as far as they were concerned and unless it was threatened they hardly noticed it at all.

But while the white people were saying "It has always been this way," the Negro people were beginning to wonder whether it need always remain the same. Many of their sons and daughters had gone away to college and when they came back they seemed to think that the fact of being an American should overshadow the fact of being a Negro;

some had lived in the North for several years and were unwilling to readjust to the Southern way of life. These young
people were "new Negroes" who not only knew what they
wanted but hoped to get it. They told their parents that
there could be another way of life for Negroes, and their
parents began to believe them.

Montgomery, in 1954, faced in two directions; it looked
forward to a future of growth and economic expansion and,
at the same time, it looked over its shoulder to the past. Its
white people clung to a romantic memory of a gracious
plantation way of life, to a vision of an imaginary world
peopled with gallant, courteous white masters and gay and
contented colored slaves. Looking backward they failed to
notice that the Negro people they had once known and understood had ceased to exist.

During his student days Martin Luther King had made
what he called "an intellectual pilgrimage to nonviolence."
He came to Montgomery at a time when a strong undercur-
rent of Negro resentment seethed beneath a calm surface of
"peace between the races" and a year after his arrival Mrs.
Parks's arrest roused the city's Negroes to action. Was it
coincidence or was it the inscrutable forces of history that
fused together a people who were ready to protest and a
man who was ready to lead them in a peaceful rebellion?
King thinks it was neither. He believes that a superhuman
influence guided the Negro people; he is convinced that God
chose Montgomery to bring the message of nonviolence to
America. "In the struggle for righteousness," he has said,
"man has cosmic companionship."

Whatever the reasons, it was soon apparent that Henry
Thoreau's peaceable revolution, declared with so little effect

in Concord, Massachusetts, and waged so successfully and courageously by Gandhi and the Indian people, had once more crossed the seas and come back to America. In Montgomery the American Negro served peaceful notice that the days of his unprotesting servitude were numbered.

4

Opposition

THE WHITE PEOPLE of Montgomery counted on the first rainy day to dampen the Negroes' spirits and send them hurrying back to the buses. But when the heavens opened up and every inch of space in the colored taxis and car-pools was filled, the rest of the Negro people made it clear that they preferred the dignified shelter of their umbrellas to the indignities they had known on the buses. It was on that day, when hundreds of Negroes walked in the rain, that the white community began to take the protest seriously.

City officials made their first move to fight the boycott by putting an end to the Negro taxi system of cheap transportation; they announced that a law requiring taxi drivers to collect 45¢ minimum fares would be strictly enforced. But the boycotters seemed to step right over this first obstacle placed in their path. Hundreds of Negro automobile-owning volunteers hurried to fill the void left by the taxis. Ministers, housewives, teachers, businessmen and laborers formed a mammoth car-pool and drove carefully worked out routes to and from forty-eight dispatch and forty-two pickup stations throughout the city. White housewives, wanting their domestic workers to keep their accustomed hours or unwilling to see a loved servant walk long distances to and from the car-pool stations, aided the protest by calling for their Negro maids and cooks and driving them home at night. These white women could not, however, be counted as converts to the idea of desegregation and many of them tried to convince their servants that the protest was a bad thing for everyone concerned.

"Isn't this boycott terrible?" one wealthy employer asked her elderly Negro domestic.

"Yes, ma'am," the old woman replied, "it sure is. And I just told all my young 'uns that this kind of thing is white folks' business and we just stay off the buses till they get this whole thing settled."

Money was a problem for a while but not for long. Money was needed for organizational expenses and money poured in — at first only from the Negroes of Montgomery, but soon, as news of the protest began to spread all over the world, contributions began to come in from as far away as Japan. NAACP chapters throughout the United States helped to finance the boycott and Americans of all colors and classes sent money because they believed that something worth while was happening in Montgomery.

A week after Mrs. Parks's arrest, a meeting between Negro leaders, bus company representatives and city officials was called and came to nothing. The bus company maintained that it could not change the seating arrangements on the buses without breaking local segregation laws and made it clear that it had no intention of hiring Negro drivers. At a second meeting no progress was made and at a third, when the bus company announced that it could grant nothing more than a guarantee of driver courtesy, the mayor terminated the discussions by promising to call still another meeting at a later date. That meeting never materialized.

Opposition to the boycott then became more determined. Rumors of "settlements" and divisions within Negro ranks spread through the city, and when these failed to break up the protest, city officials embarked on a campaign designed to make life as difficult as possible for the boycotters. The mayor publicly promised to "stop pussyfooting around with the boycott" and appealed to white employers to stop taxiing

Negro domestics to and from their work. All three city commissioners announced that they had joined a White Citizens
Council, and Negro car-pool drivers, King among them, were
harassed by a series of arrests for minor or imagined traffic
violations.

Threats and warnings had been coming in by mail and
telephone to Negro leaders ever since the start of the protest
and as the first weeks passed they increased in volume and
intensity. As president of the Montgomery Improvement
Association, King bore the brunt of the attack; by the middle
of January, when the boycott was six weeks old, he was
receiving thirty to forty warnings a day. Some were relatively mild — one anonymous note reminded Montgomery's
Negroes that "God do not intend the White People and the
Negro to go to gather if he did we would be the same,"
others combined anti-Negro and anti-Semitic sentiments and
many threatened King with bodily harm. One night, toward
the end of January, the telephone rang just as he was dropping off to sleep. When he picked up the receiver he heard
an ominous voice say "Listen, nigger, we've taken all we
want from you; before next week you'll be sorry you ever
came to Montgomery." In the face of the hatred and malice
that oozed out of these doom-filled messages, King was hard
put to maintain his composure. He began to worry about
Coretta and his baby daughter, Yolanda.

On Monday evening, January 30th, King left his house a
little before seven o'clock to speak at a mass meeting at Ralph
Abernathy's First Baptist Church. Because of the unending
stream of threats, he had made it a practice never to leave
Coretta alone and that particular evening Mrs. Mary Lucy
Williams, a member of King's congregation, had come to the
parsonage to stay with Coretta and the baby. Soon after
King left, Coretta put the baby to sleep in a bedroom at the

back of the house and, after she and Mrs. Williams had chatted for a while, they went into the living room to watch television. At about nine-thirty they were startled by the sound of an object dropping on the front porch. Frightened, the two women ran to the back of the house to where the baby was sleeping. Seconds later, the house was rocked by an explosion. If, instead of running to the baby, they had gone to investigate the noise, Coretta and Mrs. Williams might well have been killed. A bomb had gone off on the front porch.

King, helping to take the collection at the close of the mass meeting, looked up and saw an usher whispering to Ralph Abernathy. Abernathy hurried away and disappeared. Several people rushed into the church and spoke to members of the congregation. All at once it seemed to King that everyone looked worried and upset and when Abernathy reappeared he called to him to ask what was the matter. Abernathy had wanted to keep the news of the bombing from him until it had been learned whether his wife and baby were safe, but now he quietly told King what had happened. King turned and spoke to the congregation. He told them about the bombing and asked them to remain calm and to remember their pledge to nonviolence. Then he hurried out of the church and was driven to his home.

He found a crowd of angry Negro people milling around in his front yard and surrounding his house. Policemen were pushing and shoving in an attempt to clear the street, but the enraged mob ignored them. When policemen tried to reassure the crowd that they would protect the Reverend Mr. King from any further harm, someone in the crowd yelled, "But who's going to protect the pastor from you?" Rushing into the house King was overwhelmed with relief and gratitude when he saw that Coretta and the baby and

Mrs. Williams were unharmed. Coretta was amazingly calm. She was so thankful that no one had been hurt that she refused to give way to panic, and King, recovering from his fright, drew strength from her composure.

The mayor and the police commissioner had hurried to the bombing scene and now they, together with several newspaper reporters, were standing in the dining room waiting for King. When he came in to speak to them both the mayor and the commissioner hastened to assure him of their deep regret that such a terrible thing had happened in Montgomery. Their hypocrisy was too much for one of the trustees of King's church who was standing nearby. Emboldened by the crisis, he turned to the mayor and said, "You may express your regrets but you must face the fact that your public statements created the atmosphere for this bombing. This is the end result of your 'get-tough' policy." The Negroes in the room waited anxiously for the mayor's answer, but he had no answer — he turned his eyes away from their gaze.

Outside the sounds from the angry crowd rose and fell. The police were having more and more difficulty controlling the constantly growing mob, and rumors were going around that some of the Negroes who had rushed to the scene were armed. Inside the house the mayor and the police commissioner were ready to leave and the newspaper reporters were anxious to get away to file their stories, but all of them were obviously apprehensive about leaving the safety of the house.

The scene inevitably calls to mind Gandhi's narrow escape from the fury of a mob in Natal. Barricaded in the house of a friend, he finally made his escape in disguise while the police commissioner distracted the attention of the milling crowd of angry whites outside. In Montgomery the cast of the drama was almost the same, but some of the roles were reversed. This time the mob was black and it was the police commissioner who was afraid to step outside.

Hoping to ease the tension, King took the mayor and the commissioner out onto the shattered porch of the parsonage and together the three men looked out on the sea of resentful faces spotlit by police searchlights. As King gestured for quiet the jeers and sullen mutters of the crowd slowly subsided. Quietly, the minister told the assembled people that he was safe and that his wife and child were unharmed. "Now let's not become panicky," he continued. "If you have weapons, take them home; if you do not have them, please do not seek to get them. We cannot solve this problem through retaliatory violence. We must meet violence with nonviolence . . . We must love our white brothers no matter what they do to us. We must make them know that we love them. Jesus still cries out in words that echo across the centuries: 'Love your enemies; bless them that curse you; pray for them that despitefully use you.' This is what we must live by . . ."

As King spoke, many of his listeners unabashedly wept. The bombing of their pastor's home had frightened them and had opened the gates of hostility in their hearts. Now, standing amid the bomb debris, King was asking them to forgive the white men who had put his family in danger. When King stopped speaking a call rang out from the crowd, "We're with you all the way, Reverend!" and hundreds of people roared "Amen." But when the police commissioner stepped forward and tried to speak, his voice was lost in a chorus of boos. Again King gestured for quiet and when the jeers died down the commissioner made a short speech in which he offered a reward for the apprehension of the bombers. Then the crowd dispersed and, though the battle lines for a race riot had been clearly drawn and nerves had been stretched to the breaking point, Montgomery passed the crisis without further violence.

But fear would not yet loosen its grip on Martin and Coretta King. Spending the night at the home of one of their church members, they found it hard to fall asleep and then, sometime past midnight, they were awakened by the sound of a steady knocking on the front door of the house. In *Stride Toward Freedom*, King tells of how panic, so carefully restrained earlier in the evening, now welled up in the darkness and threatened to engulf them:

> . . . We looked at each other wordlessly in the dim light, and listened as the knocking began again. Through the window we could see the dark outline of a figure on the front porch. Our hosts were sound asleep in the back of the house and we lay in the front, frozen into inaction. Eventually the sounds stopped and we saw a shadowy figure move across the porch and start down the steps to the street. I pulled myself out of bed, peered through the curtains, and recognized the stocky, reassuring back of Coretta's father . . .

Obie Scott had heard of the bombing on a news broadcast and had driven the eighty miles from his home in Marion to take his daughter and granddaughter back with him to safety. But though her father pleaded with her, Coretta would not leave her husband, and Obie Scott drove back to Marion alone.

The bombing shocked not only the Negro people but many whites as well. In the days that followed, some white people dropped in at King's house to offer their sympathy, and notes of encouragement, unsigned or signed simply "A White Friend," began to trickle into the office of the Montgomery Improvement Association. Once, when a big black Cadillac driven by a white man pulled up sharply in front of a car-pool pickup station, the Negro people waiting there stepped back in fear only to hear the driver call out to them, "I hope you people stay off the buses — once you go back you'll never win." It was obvious that the white community was not solidly opposed to the Negroes' aims, but no white group publicly spoke out in their support.

Soon after the bombing the opposition stepped up its campaign to defeat the boycott. A Montgomery County Grand Jury, called on February 13th to consider the bus boycott, found it illegal and in a show of strength indicted 115 of the protest's leaders and key workers on a charge of breaking a state anti-boycott law. City officials, obviously hoping that the indictment would jolt the city's Negroes into submission, were confounded when a stream of the Negro community's most respected citizens cheerfully presented themselves for arrest. Some Negroes called the sheriff's office to see if their names were on the list of those indicted and expressed disappointment when told that they were not. The arrested Negroes were released on bond and their trial was set for March 19th.

Radio commentators, television crewmen and reporters of the national and world press converged on Montgomery. Leaders of the opposing sides in the bus controversy were interviewed, photographed and quoted, and by the opening day of the trial the attention of the whole nation and many other parts of the world was focused on the dingy Mont-gomery courthouse.

King was the first defendant and during the four days that his case was heard a huge crowd of Negroes, many of them wearing lapel pins that read "Father Forgive Them," filled the little courtroom and overflowed into the halls and the surrounding streets. A succession of defense witnesses, many of them uneducated and obviously frightened, haltingly told of the humiliations and brutalities they had suffered on the city buses. The prosecution tried to prove that the drivers were generally courteous to Negro passengers. When all the evidence was in, King believed that the Negro story had been presented so well that there was reason to hope for a favorable decision. But if Judge Eugene Carter believed that the Negroes had the stronger case he was unable to face the inevitable censure from the white community that would follow acquittal. Almost immediately, he returned a verdict of "guilty" and imposed a penalty of $500 and court costs, or 386 days at hard labor. King's lawyers announced that they would appeal the case, his bond was signed and he was released. The judge postponed the trial of the other accused Negroes pending the outcome of King's appeal.

If the decision of guilty was aimed at cowing the Negro people into submission it fell far short of its mark. As King walked out of the courthouse he was greeted by hundreds of voices singing "We Ain't Gonna Ride the Buses No More."

In the newspapers and on radio and television America took a long look at the boycott. This was obviously a people's movement. King was its principal spokesman and he shared the spotlight with several other key boycott figures: Ralph Abernathy, E. D. Nixon and Robert Graetz, the white minister of the Negro Trinity Lutheran Church, were among the score or more men and women who, together with King, organized and encouraged Montgomery's Negroes, but it was clear that these leaders were only guiding a course of action that had sprung directly from the Negro people themselves. The continuing strength of the boycott in the face of determined opposition from the white community was clear-cut evidence that the Negro people were capable of resolute and determined resistance to oppression. Led by clergymen and conducted by masses of law-abiding citizens the protest was maintained on a high moral plane.

Mass nonviolent resistance was a new and fascinating spectacle to the American people. The newspaper photographs of Negroes trudging to their work reminded many Americans of pictures they had seen of Gandhi's Salt March to the Sea. It seemed to them that much that was meaningful to all Americans was at stake in Montgomery — that on the city's crowded pavements justice warred with injustice and the past wrestled with the future.

Martin Luther King pulls up a cross that was burned on his front lawn. With him is his son, Martin Luther King III.

White teen-agers mock Negro pickets in front of a lunch counter.

A Negro demonstrator is pulled from the doorway of a restaurant
where a "stand-in" attempt is going on.

Two college students quietly do their homework at an all-white
lunch counter as waitresses look on.

A fourteen-year old manfully munches on a sandwich to test the reaction at a lunch counter that has just been integrated.

A Freedom Rider bus goes up in flames at Anniston, Georgia.

Freedom Riders proudly sing hymns on their way to jail.

5

Victory and Terror

MARCH, APRIL, MAY — hardly anyone had to walk now. Contributions to the Montgomery Improvement Association had been so heavy that the organization had been able to buy fifteen new station wagons to enlarge its car-pool. Twenty-five drivers worked full-time for six days each week and trained dispatchers stood at car-pool stations to divide groups according to where the waiting people were heading. The car-pool kept to its schedule with military precision and yet some Negroes who didn't live impossibly long distances from their jobs chose to walk even when a ride was available. The lovely spring weather had something to do with it. It was pleasant to walk along and smell the blossoming trees and stop to talk to a friend, but it was something more than that. By walking, colored people in Montgomery felt as though they were doing something active for their cause. Once, when a shiny car-pool station wagon stopped to pick up an elderly woman walking on a city sidewalk she waved the car on. "I want to walk now," she called out to the driver, "so my children and grandchildren can ride the buses."

Negro spirits drooped occasionally but they were quickly revived at the twice-weekly mass meetings held in each of the city's Negro churches in turn. Sitting in the crowded pews and overflowing into the aisles Negroes of every religious denomination and from every rung of the economic ladder drew encouragement and strength from each other as they listened to their leaders urge them to express the teachings of their religion in nonviolent resistance. The

name of Mohandas Gandhi rang out in Negro churches and
as they heard the story of the hard-won Satyagraha struggle,
Negro men and women who had never traveled beyond
the boundaries of their city felt a kinship with the Indian
people across the sea.

Early in the spring, boycott leaders gave up hope of getting the concessions they had requested, concessions they
believed could be granted to them well within the limitations of Montgomery's segregation laws and customs. Having been refused the inch they asked, they set their sights
higher and went after the whole mile; they filed suit in
Federal Court calling for the end of bus segregation and
for the prevention of city officials' interference with Negro
civil rights. Thus Montgomery's Negroes shifted from a
protest against an unjust application of segregation laws to
an attack on segregation itself.

In June a three-judge Federal Court panel declared that
the city bus segregation laws of Alabama were unconstitutional. It was a joyful moment for the Negroes but the city's
attorneys promptly announced that they would appeal the
decision to the Supreme Court and the boycott leaders knew
that the battle was yet to be won.

In still another move to break up the boycott, the city
officials filed an action at the end of October against the
Negroes' car-pool, charging that it was obstructing the business of the bus company, and a hearing on the action was
called for November 13th. This time the protest leaders
were seriously worried; if the car-pool was outlawed some
Negroes might be forced to go back to the buses. Just when
there was real hope for success it seemed that all the work
and sacrifice might have been in vain. Try as he might,
King could see no way out.

Sitting at a table at the front of the courthouse, King, the chief defendant for the car-pool, was filled with gloom. The hearing was being held before the same judge who had found King guilty of breaking an anti-boycott law and there was no reason to hope that he would see the Negroes' case more objectively this time. The proceedings dragged on — the prosecution charging that the car-pool was a "public nuisance" and the defense maintaining that since it was a nonprofit venture it had a right to operate. And then all at once there was a stir in the courtroom. The mayor and the police commissioner hurried to the back of the room where they huddled in conference with the city attorneys. Something was evidently amiss. The mystery was cleared up for King when a reporter came up to him and handed him a piece of paper, saying "Here is the decision you have been waiting for." Relief flooded over King as he read. That same day the Supreme Court had ruled the Alabama state and local laws requiring segregation on the buses to be unconstitutional.

Hurrying over to where Ralph Abernathy, E. D. Nixon and Coretta were sitting, King told them the good news and soon the word spread and smiles appeared on every Negro face in the courtroom. "God Almighty has spoken from Washington, D.C.," exulted one excited spectator. The interrupted hearing resumed but King no longer cared what the outcome might be. The car-pool might be outlawed but the need for it had, that day, melted away.

Judge Carter, true to expectations, ruled that the car-pool was illegal. His decision created some difficulties for the city's Negroes, for at a mass meeting held that night they decided to stay off the buses until the official Supreme Court order arrived from Washington. However, knowing that the end of the road was in sight, some Negroes announced that they would walk the rest of the way and the others cooperated in setting up neighborhood share-the-ride schemes.

While they waited for the court order to reach Montgomery, Negro leaders devoted all their energies to preparing their people for desegregated bus riding. Throughout the city Negroes received mimeographed lists of "Suggestions for Integrating Buses" instructing them to "Remember that this is not a victory for Negroes alone, but for all Montgomery and the South. Do not boast; Do not brag! . . ." They were asked to be "quiet but friendly; proud but not arrogant; joyous but not boisterous . . . be loving enough to absorb evil and understanding enough to turn an enemy into a friend." Specific suggestions included:

> Do not deliberately sit by a white person, unless there is no other seat.
>
> If cursed, do not curse back. If pushed, do not push back. If struck, do not strike back, but evidence love and goodwill at all times.
>
> According to your own ability and personality, do not be afraid to experiment with new and creative techniques for achieving reconciliation and social change.
>
> If you feel you cannot take it, walk for another week or two. . . .

In Negro churches rows of chairs were set up in front of the altars to simulate the interiors of buses and, playing the roles of hostile white men and women, some church members tried to provoke Negro "passengers" in order to test their resources of nonviolence. Harsh, angry words rang out and shattered the peaceful quiet of the churches. "Here you nigger! Get to the back of the bus!" shouted a "white" man while another tried to pull a "Negro" out of his chair: "I wouldn't ever sit next to a black ape," haughtily announced a "white" woman as she stood over an empty chair and glared at the colored woman sitting next to it. This was not just play-acting — it was deadly serious business and some of the actors were so carried away by their roles that more than once a "Negro" had to be bodily restrained from assaulting a "white" man. The Negro people knew that they needed this practice in nonviolence; discipline, dignity, forgiveness — these had to be their watchwords in the months that lay ahead.

Unfortunately, the white community made no preparation at all for peaceful integration of the buses. All through the protest the white people of Montgomery had allowed their city officials to speak for them and, even after the Supreme Court decision, no white group was willing to become involved in "such a controversial issue." One group of businessmen, the Men of Montgomery, did draft out a statement calling for courtesy and a peaceful approach to the new situation but some of its membership blocked its publication. The three city commissioners seemed to be deliberately trying to heighten the tension that gripped the city as it awaited the desegregation of its buses; they publicly promised to do all in their power "to oppose the integration of the Negro race with the white race in Montgomery" and "to stand like a rock against social equality." A White Citizens Council leader added his coals to the fire of white hostility by predicting that "any attempt to enforce this [Supreme Court] decision will lead to riot and bloodshed."

The court order finally reached Montgomery on December 20th. That night King addressed a mass meeting and made his final plea for good will and restraint:

> . . . We must respond to the decision with an understanding of those who have oppressed us and with an appreciation of the new adjustments that the court

order poses for them. We must be able to face up honestly to our own shortcomings. We must act in such a way to make possible a coming together of white people and colored people on the basis of a real harmony of interests and understanding . . . Violence must not come from any of us, for if we become victimized with violent intents, we will have walked in vain, and our twelve months of glorious dignity will be transformed into an eve of gloomy catastrophe. . . .

The first day of bus integration went deceptively well. Trailed by a bevy of reporters and photographers, King, together with Abernathy, Nixon and Glenn Smiley, a white minister friendly to the Negro cause, boarded a bus near his home at 6 A.M. The white driver smiled at King and told him, "We are glad to have you this morning," and there were pleased expressions on the faces of the other passengers. Later, when the group transferred to a bus that followed a route through a predominantly white neighborhood, there were some signs of hostility but no major incidents. One white man, noticing the Negroes sitting in the front of the bus, ignored the vacant seats farther back and defiantly stood just behind the driver; "I'd rather die and go to hell than sit behind a nigger," he told a reporter. A woman jumped up hastily when she saw that her seatmate was colored and one white man slapped a Negro woman as she got off the bus. Schooled to expect these incidents, the Negroes took them in stride. And countering the unpleasantness was the joy of discovering the friendliness of other white people who deliberately sat down next to Negroes to demonstrate their acceptance of the new situation.

But violence had been predicted by city officials and segregationist groups, and as if to oblige them, violence broke out. One night as a bus carrying Negroes drove through an unpopulated and poorly lit section of the city a sniper's rifle bullets crashed against its sides. Within the next few days a Negro teen-age girl was beaten at a deserted bus stop, a Negro woman was shot in the leg and other buses were fired on. Many of Montgomery's citizens, both colored and white, were afraid to ride the buses.

On the night of January 9th, King and Abernathy, in Atlanta for a meeting of Southern Negro leaders, were awakened by a phone call at 2 A.M. It was Abernathy's wife, Juanita, reporting the awful news that their house had been bombed and that several other explosions had been heard in the city. Juanita Abernathy was able to assure her husband that neither she nor their daughter had been hurt, but before the night was over more bad news had traveled over the wires to Atlanta: King and Abernathy learned that Abernathy's church, three other Negro Baptist churches and the home of their white friend, the Reverend Robert Graetz, had also been bombed.

The two ministers took the first plane back to Montgomery, hoping against hope that they would be in time to help restrain the Negro community's anger at the latest terrorist attack. They found that both Abernathy's and Graetz's houses had been severely damaged and that two of the bombed churches had been completely destroyed. Crowds of saddened Negroes stood and stared at the ruins of the homes and churches, but they made no move to retaliate.

The bombings shocked some of Montgomery's white citizens into action. Several white ministers denounced the violence as uncivilized and un-Christian, the editor of the *Montgomery Advertiser* pointed out that the city had been seriously degraded by the segregationists' lawlessness and the

Men of Montgomery made it clear that they opposed a defense of segregation by terror. However, it wasn't until three more bombings had shaken the city that official action was taken. An investigation was ordered, rewards were offered for information leading to the apprehension of the bombers and, on the last day of January, seven white men were arrested in connection with the attacks. But the principle of white supremacy was still the overriding law in Montgomery. Charges against two of the men were dropped and, despite the fact that the other five had signed confessions, at the trial of the first two defendants the jury returned a verdict of "not guilty."

Strangely, though justice had obviously miscarried, the trial saw the end of the violent resistance to bus integration; from that time forward Montgomery's white and colored people rode the desegregated buses without incident. The leaders of the Negro community, however, were under no illusions. They knew that long-standing fears and prejudices could not be quickly washed away, that the Negro people's victory was still incomplete. Nevertheless, they rejoiced when they counted the important gains that had been made.

The Negro people had found in nonviolence a moral and effective way of resisting their oppressors. They had found new dignity and pride, and fear was losing its grip on them. The white people of Montgomery, having suffered neither bodily harm nor property damage, were able, without bitterness, to offer the city's Negro citizens a cautious new respect; faced with the accomplished fact of bus desegregation many white people privately admitted their admiration of the Negroes' courage, restraint and organizational ability.

State and local politicians continued to be as active as ever in their efforts to protect the people of Alabama from the "dangers" of integration, and the White Citizens Councils continued to send out their messages of hate and fear, but there was no gainsaying the fact that a subtle change had taken place; one striking indication of the change was a steady decrease in contributions to Montgomery's White Citizens Council.

6

The Turning Point at Little Rock

NONVIOLENT RESISTANCE had triumphed in Montgomery and the white South hoped that that was the end of it, but for the Negro people, it had just begun.

Everywhere in the South, Negro groups were joining a new organization, the Southern Christian Leadership Conference, based in Atlanta, and headed by Martin Luther King. The full integration of American society was the Conference's aim, "creative protest" was its rallying call, and nonviolence was the method it preached. The SCLC called on all Americans to oppose segregation as an evil that acted against not only Negro but also white citizens by preventing the United States from taking its rightful place as a world leader. The Conference, based on "Hebraic-Christian tradition coupled with the Gandhian concept of satyagraha," called for nonviolent resistance to all forms of racial injustice and planned its major attack against segregation in the field of Negro voting. On the one hand, the SCLC would try to overcome the numerous obstacles placed in the path of Negroes seeking to register and vote, and on the other hand, it would encourage all Negroes who could register unopposed to do so. Negro equality would never become a reality, the SCLC reminded its members, until Negroes became as concerned about their responsibilities as they were about their rights.

Another organization, CORE, the Congress on Racial Equality, also aimed at the defeat of segregation through nonviolent action. Among its leaders were men who had been to India and had studied the life and philosophy of

Mohandas Gandhi. CORE and SCLC leaders, trained in the techniques of nonviolence, traveled all over the South addressing Negro groups and holding clinics and training sessions. Noncooperation and civil disobedience together with the names of Thoreau and Gandhi were becoming household words in thousands of Negro homes.

At the same time American Negroes were watching events across the sea. Africa, their ancestral homeland, was shaking off the chains of colonial rule and demanding its freedom from white domination. In the period between the end of the Second World War and 1957, five African nations had gained their independence and black Africans were sitting at conference tables with white world leaders and stating their cases in the forum of the United Nations. When, suddenly, the name of Little Rock, Arkansas, filled the headlines of the world's press, these same black Africans pointed out, none too gently, to the Americans who were wooing their friendship, the glaring discrepancies between American ideals of freedom and American practice.

On May 17, 1954, Chief Justice Warren, speaking for the United States Supreme Court, had said, "We conclude that in the field of public education, the doctrine of 'separate but equal' has no place. Separate educational facilities are inherently unequal." In the high court's ruling that segregation in the public schools was unconstitutional, American Negroes saw what Martin Luther King called "the exit sign to freedom" — for the first time they had concrete reason to hope that they need not indefinitely accept a second-class status. But, in the fall of 1957, their hopes faded into frustration and despair: in several Southern cities, notably in Little Rock, white mobs roamed the streets in angry defiance of the highest law of the land.

For two years the State of Arkansas had successfully

avoided compliance with the school desegregation order, but in 1957 last-minute appeals for further delay were refused by a federal district court and nine Negro boys and girls were assigned to enter Little Rock's Central High School at the beginning of the fall term. Governor Orval Faubus set the tone for white reaction to the forthcoming token desegregation by publicly announcing that violence and bloodshed would surely follow any attempt to integrate Central High; his prophecy was taken up and repeated by a chorus of local segregationist groups, prejudices and fears were carefully stimulated and nourished, and anti-Negro sentiment spread through the city like a disease.

In a Little Rock home a group of women gathered over coffee and listened as their indignant hostess said, "It'll be the beginning of the end for our kids. Those Negroes are dirty and ignorant and they'll pull down all the standards of the school." Another woman put down her coffee cup and quietly announced, "No matter what those old men in Washington say, I know I'm not letting my daughter go to school and sit next to any nigger."

"Our colored folk were satisfied before," a white Southerner assured a businessman from the North. "It's that NAACP that riled 'em up to look for what they don't really want. It's too bad — the colored and white people used to get along fine here."

"Maybe the NAACP thinks they're gonna get away with it," said one burly white man, "but I know a lot of people in this town that say they're not."

And so the talk went as the opening day of school approached. There were white people in Little Rock who were willing to accept the high court's decision but they were careful to conceal their feelings on the subject: they were frightened by the juggernaut of hatred that careened through the city threatening to cut down anyone, white or black, who tried to stop its course. On the eve of the first day of school Governor Faubus acted "to preserve the peace" by sending over 200 state militiamen to patrol Central High School. But peace was not so easily ensured and justice, it appeared, had fled the city.

By 8 A.M. of the day that the Negro students were scheduled to enter Central High a crowd of about 400 white people had gathered across the street from the school. The rifle-bearing State Guardsmen who walked up and down the street eyed them watchfully but made no attempt to disperse them. Suddenly, as someone spotted fifteen-year-old Elizabeth Eckford slowly approaching, a cry rang out, "A nigger! They're coming!" and the crowd, united by bonds of hate, screamed, "Nigger go home! Go back where you came from!" Trembling, Elizabeth climbed the steps to the entrance of the school only to find that the soldier stationed there had been instructed not to guarantee the Negro students safe conduct, but to bar them from the school. With the shouts and taunts of the raging crowd ringing in her ears, the colored girl slowly walked down the steps and over to a bench at a nearby bus stop where she sat, bewildered and stunned. A white woman who pushed her way through the crowd and hurried over to the girl to comfort her was trailed by a chorus of jeers and shouts of "Nigger-lover!" Elizabeth's experience convinced the other eight Negro boys and girls that there was no use in trying to go to school that day.

The next morning Negroes all over the South saw undisguised hostility staring at them from newspaper photographs of hate-contorted white faces. A shocked world found it hard to believe that the picture they saw in their papers of a rifle-bearing soldier standing between a Negro girl and her school was taken in America, "the land of the free and the home of the brave."

Acting on the advice of the NAACP, the Negro students stayed away from Central High until after Governor Faubus reluctantly responded to an order of the federal government and withdrew the National Guardsmen on September 21st. Three days later, when the Negro boys and girls were scheduled to return, the white mob was again on hand and this time there was nothing to stand between them and the objects of their rage. But the Negro students managed to slip into the school through a side door, and when the mob outside learned that it had been outwitted, its fury exploded. While hysterical white parents stormed into the school to get their children and take them home, the fanatical crowd kicked, cuffed and beat newspapermen who were covering the scene and Negroes who happened to be passing nearby. Before long interracial brawling had spread through the city.

President Eisenhower had reached the limit of his patience. He immediately sent 1000 troops of the 101st Airborne Division to the city "to prevent mob rule and anarchy." For the next month the steel-helmeted paratroopers escorted the Negro boys and girls in and out of the school and they remained in the city for the remainder of the school term, keeping crowds from congregating near Central High and patrolling the corridors of the school.

Little Rock seethed with resentment. Its citizens saw their city "invaded" by the federal government, their state's rights overridden by the will of the Supreme Court. The federal soldiers stationed outside the school effectively ruled out any further mob violence but the segregationists' fury crept past their surveillance and entered the school with the white students; there was little the paratroopers could do to protect the Negro boys and girls from the harassment meted out to them by some of their white schoolmates.

In the crowded hallways an elbow jabbed painfully and none of the white faces showed a change of expression; a foot was stuck out in the path of a Negro boy or girl and it was impossible to tell whose foot it was; a low voice hissed, "Nigger, go back to Africa," and only the ears they were intended for heard the words; day after day tacks were carefully placed point-up on the colored students' chairs; hot soup was "inadvertently" spilled on them at lunchtime and the Negro boys and girls learned to be especially careful on the stairways where "accidents" were most likely to occur.

Though only about 5 per cent of the white boys and girls at Central High took part in this systematic campaign of intimidation, the teen-age segregationists imposed their reign of terror not only on the Negro students but also on those white boys and girls who showed any inclination to be friendly to them. The names of white students who smiled at the Negroes or who spoke to them were promptly reported to segregationist groups outside the school and anonymous threatening phone calls were made to the parents of the "nigger-lovers." Most people are not brave; white boys and girls were carefully instructed by frightened parents to stay as far away from the Negroes as possible. As a result the colored boys and girls found themselves completely isolated from all their white schoolmates; as they walked through the halls they were studiously ignored and in the cafeteria they sat together at a table that was "reserved" for them by the white students, who avoided it as they would the plague. They saw a few unmistakable signs of white friendliness, but these were always furtive and the newcomers knew that they were made at considerable risk.

The Negro boys and girls didn't give up. They stayed at Central High and their courage and endurance were marveled at throughout the country. At an age when friends, fun and being accepted in a group are especially important, they took constant ridicule, harassment and rejection without striking back and without becoming unduly bitter. (There was one exception. Goaded beyond her endurance, one girl did retaliate. She was expelled from Central High and spent the rest of the year as a scholarship student at a New York City private school.) The teen-age Negroes knew that they were pioneers, that they were blazing an easier way for their younger sisters and brothers and they were proud that, young as they were, they were heroes to the Negro people. They tried hard to remember that many of their white classmates would have liked to make them feel more welcome. One girl proudly told a reporter about a white girl who always managed "to be nice" but wouldn't tell her name "because she's already had trouble"; a Negro boy told of receiving notes from white students "telling me to keep my chin up."

When school closed for the year, segregationist agitation increased in the city, and the following September Governor Faubus ordered the closing of all four of the city's high schools. They remained closed for the entire school year and the high-school-age boys and girls of Little Rock attended makeshift classes set up by their parents in private homes or went away to schools in other cities or filled their time as best they could by going to movies and hanging around drugstores and lunch counters. For some the impact of what had happened was slow in coming: "It was a terrible thing to have happen what with the football team winning," said one pretty blond girl; but for those whose plans for going to college were set back a year and for others who were sensitive to the hate and bitterness that swirled around them, the violence in their city and the subsequent closing of the schools left scars that were a long time in healing.

To Negroes all over the South, Little Rock meant pain, resentment and frustration. With the prospect of school desegregation they had seen first-class citizenship appear on the horizon; with the hostility of the white mobs in Little Rock they saw their hopes for equality indefinitely postponed. A poem by the Negro poet Langston Hughes poses a question that was troubling many Negroes in those days.

> *What happens to a dream deferred?*
>   *Does it dry up*
>   *like a raisin in the sun?*
>   *Or fester like a sore —*
>   *And then run?*
>   *Or does it stink like rotten meat?*
>   *Or crust and sugar over*
>   *like a syrupy sweet?*
>
> *Maybe it just sags*
> *like a heavy load.*
>
> Or does it explode?

Negro leaders protested the continuing denial of Negro rights. Petitions were filed and mass prayer meetings were held. Martin Luther King and other Negro leaders met first with Vice President Nixon and later with President Eisenhower but almost nothing was accomplished. While the NAACP continued to depend on court action and public education in its attack on injustice, many of the younger generations of Negroes grew impatient with its gradual approach; Henry Thoreau might have been speaking for them when he said in "Civil Disobedience": "As for adopting the ways which the state has provided for remedying the evil,

I know not of such ways. They take too much time and a man's life will be gone." Wanting to participate actively in the fight against segregation, many young Negroes were seriously considering Mohandas Gandhi's prescription for rebellion:

> . . . things of fundamental importance to the people are not secured by reason alone, but have to be purchased with their suffering. . . . Nobody has perhaps drawn up more petitions or espoused more forlorn causes than I, and I have come to the fundamental conclusion that if you want something really important to be done you must not merely satisfy the reason, you must move the heart also . . . the penetration of the heart comes from suffering. It opens the inner understanding of men.

The time was ripe, the method and the weapon were at hand. The white South, trying to forget the violence at Little Rock, looked around and, seeing "peaceful relations between the races," hoped for the best. The black South knew that there was more to come.

7

The Sit-Ins

At 4:45 on the afternoon of February 1, 1960, four young men, freshman students at North Carolina Agricultural and Technical College, entered a variety store on Elm Street in downtown Greensboro. During the next few minutes, while they bought toothpaste and stationery supplies at several of the counters, there was nothing to distinguish them from the rest of the crowd of colored and white customers. But when they went over to the soda fountain, sat down and asked for a cup of coffee, they made history: sitting at the soda fountain they issued a direct challenge to the time-honored social system of the South.

The waitress behind the counter put the store's policy succinctly. "I'm sorry," she said, "but we don't serve colored here."

Though it was common practice in Southern cities for Negroes and whites to eat side by side at "stand-up" counters, the "sit-down" lunch counters in drug, department and variety stores revealed the "so far and no farther" principle that governed Southern life — their stools were reserved exclusively for white people.

"I beg your pardon," said Franklin McCain, eighteen, to the waitress. "You just served me at a counter two feet away. Why is it that you serve me at one counter and deny me at another? Why not stop serving me at all the counters?"

The waitress's answer, if any, is not recorded, but it is known that the four students sat at the soda fountain unserved until the store closed at 5:30 P.M. Planning to return the next day the four boys called the chairman of the

Greensboro chapter of the NAACP and asked if they could expect help from the organization if they needed it; they were told that they could. When twenty other North Carolina A & T college students volunteered to join the protest a set of simple ground rules was drawn up; all of the volunteers agreed to refrain from name-calling, raising their voices or protesting when they were not served.

The students thought that they would be arrested when they returned to the soda fountain, but they were treated politely by the store manager, who told them that his refusal to serve them was based not on how he felt, but on local custom. The next day the protest group was enlarged and by the end of the week there were more than 100 young Negroes sitting at the original soda fountain and at one in another Greensboro variety store. Fifty-five miles away at North Carolina College in Durham, students heard a radio broadcast about the Greensboro demonstrations and, on February 8th, started one of their own. From there the idea snowballed through Southern Negro colleges; within a month there were "sit-ins" in twenty cities in six Southern states and day after day, with monotonous regularity, the newspapers continued to report new demonstrations.

White Southerners shook their heads and worried; this was not "kid stuff," a localized bit of racial trouble that could easily be shrugged off. They looked around for "outside agitators" and found none. The sit-ins seemed to be a purely Southern movement and the adult Negro organizations — the NAACP, CORE and the SCLC — were staying in the background, confining themselves on the whole to giving aid to demonstrations that started spontaneously among the students. What lay behind it all? Just how much did these young people want? How could they be stopped?

Joseph McNeil, seventeen, and Ezell Blair, eighteen, two

of the four original Greensboro sit-ins, tried to explain to reporters why they had taken the action they had. McNeil told them that though he and his friends were only "green school kids" at the time of the Little Rock riots, the nine Negro boys and girls who had braved the segregationists' fury were idols to them. Blair said that he had given a lot of thought to a television program he had seen about India's fight for freedom. He couldn't forget the pictures he had seen of Mohandas Gandhi leaving jail only to be arrested again. He and McNeil, his roommate, spent long evenings discussing Gandhi and his Satyagraha campaign with several other boys. One Sunday night McNeil had said, "Well, we've talked about it long enough. Let's do something." He suggested trying to get a cup of coffee at one of Greensboro's segregated variety stores and the next day he, Blair, McCain and another boy, David Richmond, put the plan into action.

The idea, simple in the extreme, was symbolically just right. The exclusion of Negroes from Southern soda fountains and lunch counters was a perfect illustration of the daily rejections, humiliations and nagging inconvenience that segregation meant to Southern Negroes. "It just didn't seem right," Blair told reporters, "that we would have to walk two miles to town, buy notebook paper and toothpaste in a national chain store and then not be able to get a bite to eat and a cup of coffee." McNeil put the matter another way: "Segregation makes me feel that I'm unwanted," he said. "I don't want my children exposed to it."

It was clear that Blair and McNeil were expressing sentiments that moved thousands of Negro college students all over the South, for the sit-ins continued to spread; the spectacle of quiet, orderly Negro boys and girls sitting unwanted and unserved at lunch counters and soda fountains became commonplace in Southern cities. In almost every instance the counter at which they sat was closed by the management and signs reading *"Closed for Repairs"* or *"Closed in the Interest of Public Safety"* or *"We Reserve the Right to Service the Public as We See Fit"* were displayed. Though some of the store managers were not personally opposed to integrating their counters, all feared that if they served Negroes their white customers would boycott their stores.

And at the closed counters the students continued to sit, silent or talking quietly among themselves or studying. Crowds of white teen-agers picketed the demonstrations or stood behind the colored students, pushing and jostling and calling out insults.

"You're not wanted here, nigger, get out."

The boy sitting at the soda fountain in Nashville, Tennessee, didn't turn around. He and the colored boys and girls sitting at the counter with him stared stolidly ahead. Behind them a straggle of white boys lit cigarettes and, leaning over the Negroes' shoulders, blew smoke in their faces. When this too failed to provoke any response, one of the white boys viciously stubbed out his cigarette on a colored boy's back. The idea was catching; several others did the same. The Negroes continued to sit, unmoving. Enraged by their victims' passive acceptance of whatever was done to them, the white boys grabbed at them and pulled them off the stools. "Those of us pulled off our stools tried to regain them as soon as possible," one of the Nashville sit-ins said, "but none of us attempted to fight back in any way."

The startling contrast between the hecklers, most of whom were members of the white communities' "worst element," and the sober, dignified Negro students was described in an editorial in the Richmond, Virginia, *News Leader* of February 22nd:

> ... Many a Virginian must have felt a tinge of wry regret at the state of things as they are, in reading of Saturday's "sitdowns" by Negro students in Richmond stores. Here were the colored students, in coats, white shirts, ties, and one of them was reading Goethe and one was taking notes from a biology text. And here, on the sidewalk outside, was a gang of white boys come to heckle, a ragtail rabble, slack-jawed, black-jacketed, grinning fit to kill, and some of them, God save the mark, were waving the proud and honored flag of the Southern States in the last war fought by gentlemen. EHEU! It gives one pause.

Just how much, puzzled the white South, did these Negro college students want? Surely they were not taking so much punishment just for the privilege of drinking coffee and eating hamburgers "integrated." The white men were right. The students wanted more than that — they were aiming at the total defeat of segregation itself.

Desegregation, the students insisted, would benefit the whole South, white and black. "Look at us," they said. "We too are Southerners, we too love the South — but, restricted on all sides by segregation's laws and customs we have not been allowed to contribute to our communities and to our country; within our people lies a vast reservoir of good, waiting to be tapped.

"And," they added, "you white men stand to gain a lot more from granting us first-class citizenship. Whether you admit it or not you have been carrying a heavy burden of guilt ever since the days of slavery. Desegregation will lift that burden from your shoulders, will remove the blindfold of white supremacy from your eyes and you will be able, for the first time, to face the future realistically and un-afraid."

But most of the white South refused to listen. These were, after all, Negroes who were talking and Negroes were in-ferior human beings who must, at all costs, be kept in their place. Lowering the color bar even one notch would in-evitably lead to the destruction of the Southern way of life.

Montgomery. Winston-Salem. Tallahassee. Lexington. Little Rock. Relentlessly the sit-in movement spread out farther and farther from its base, probing deeper and deeper into the South. Always the demonstrations were peaceful and, almost without exception, the Negro students refused to strike back when harassed. Dreading a recurrence of the race riots that had shaken the South in the past, white Southerners were relieved to find that though the sit-ins were a constantly growing problem to them, surprisingly few people were getting hurt.

In each city where sit-ins occurred a group of student spokesmen approached the leaders of the white business community and suggested meetings to work out a plan for a gradual desegregation of the city's counters. Sometimes their offers were taken up and in those cities where they were rebuffed new demonstrations followed. Picketing and public prayer and song meetings supplemented the sit-ins and often adult Negroes supported their young people by boycotting segregated stores.

How could these young Negroes be stopped? Each day it became clearer that they couldn't be stopped. The old stand-by weapons of threat and intimidation didn't seem to work on them. Youth and optimism and high spirits sent fear and doubt scurrying. And, besides, there wasn't much to threaten college students with; they had no families to support or full-time jobs to lose; they were free, free to protest, free to say "We don't care what you do to us, we will eventually win."

And for many Negro students, taking part in sit-ins meant going to jail. In some cities they were breaking local segregation laws by sitting at "white" counters and in others police officials decided that they were "disturbing the peace" or "inciting to violence." But the students felt no shame as they were hustled off to jail. They were justified, they said, in breaking laws that did not apply to all Americans, laws that were in conflict with the higher law contained in the Bill of Rights. Released after serving a thirty-day sentence on a road gang for sit-in activities, Clarence Graham of Rock Hill, South Carolina, said, "If requesting first-class citizenship in the South is to be regarded as a crime, I will gladly go back to jail again."

Jail was obviously no answer to the problem the sit-ins presented to the white South. The vacant places at the counters and on the picket lines were soon filled and even inside the jails this new kind of resistance continued. The grimy, crowded cell-blocks of Southern jails resounded to the words of the sit-in movement's theme song, "We Shall Overcome." "Deep in my heart," the young voices sang over and over again, "I do believe, we shall overcome some-day."

There were white boys and girls sitting at the counters too. That was, perhaps, the most worrisome and puzzling aspect of the whole protest for white Southerners. In New Orleans a white college girl, Sissy Leonard, quietly gave police officials a hard time after she had been arrested for taking part in a sit-in. A native Southerner, obviously well-bred, she couldn't be classified as either an outsider or a radical and she stubbornly refused to be persuaded that she had been doing wrong. Later Sissy told how she tried to explain her actions:

> . . . They asked if I knew what this could lead to, and I started to tell them that I was willing to risk being kicked out of school if it had to be that way. But they didn't mean my own personal consequences; they meant damage to the community or something. I tried to explain that we thought if we did these things peacefully and refused to be violent ourselves, there wouldn't be any violence at all and that any results would be good ones.
>
> I said that I, personally, just didn't like segregation and hoped to be able to help end it. They tried, a little, to talk me out of this. They told me that no Negroes would put themselves out in any way for me, and I said yes, they would. They said only in small ways and all I could say was that they knew I felt very strongly they were wrong. . . .

In Tallahassee, Florida, six white boys from Florida State University started a sit-in by ordering coffee at a lunch counter and then giving it to six Negro boys from Florida A & M. They were all marched off to jail together, but when the cell door slammed behind them the boys began to sing and the words, "My country, 'tis of thee, sweet land of liberty," followed the policemen as they walked down the corridor of the jail. The white South dismissed their young renegades as "foolish idealists" but in many Southern cities the smattering of white faces on the picket lines and at the counters proved that for some of the younger generation interracial brotherhood had already become a reality.

Stirring up new hopes and old fears, uncovering long-stifled pride and carefully hidden doubts, the sit-ins wrote the scripts for countless dramas enacted by ordinary people.

"Try to understand that what I'm doing is right," a colored boy wrote home from college. "It isn't like going to jail for a crime . . ."

"I'm only telling you this because I'm your friend" — the white woman sat down next to the telephone and, biting her lip, she waited for the rest — ". . . it's just that your going around and telling people that you think those young niggers are right isn't going to help your husband's business any."

"It isn't ladylike to stand up to white folks," an old colored woman told her granddaughter. The girl listened respectfully and then told her grandmother that times had changed.

And in a white home up on the hill a colored cook and a white woman weren't laughing and joking together any more. The cook had worked there for twenty years and the white woman valued her service and her friendship, but the fact that the cook's son was walking a picket line had come between them.

These effects of the sit-ins were private, quiet and intangible, but when Martin Luther King urged the Negro people of the South to support the college students by "selective buying," the results were clearly recorded. "It is immoral to spend one's money where one cannot be treated with respect," King said and the effect of his words could be seen in the plummeting sales charts of many Southern retail businesses.

Nashville, Tennessee, was one city where the merchants were in a tight spot. While hundreds of young Negroes were sitting at the city's lunch counters, scores of others were walking up and down in front of the downtown stores wearing signs that read "WEAR OLD CLOTHES WITH NEW DIGNITY — DON'T BUY HERE" and the Negro people of Nashville were doing as they asked. "To most of us this whole business of sit-ins was an economic problem," one store owner said. "We knew and admitted the immorality of segregation. But we also felt and felt strongly that any integration would keep many of our regular white customers away." Acting on this belief, city businessmen sat tight and refused to integrate. But as time went on it became more and more painful for them to watch the seven million dollars that the city's Negroes normally spent annually in their stores going slowly down the drain.

The moral aspect of the problem was annoying too. Many of Nashville's white people hated to see droves of fine-looking young colored people going to jail and when the home of Z. Alexander Looby, the NAACP lawyer who defended them, was bombed one night, the explosion shook a lot more of Nashville than the ground his house stood on. Looby was very highly thought of in the white community, and later Greenfield Pitts, speaking for the city merchants, said, "I think this act did more to change the climate of community opinion than any other single factor."

And then, if there were any white people who still thought that the Negroes could be terrorized into submission, Martin Luther King changed many of their minds. He came to Nashville soon after the Looby bombing and, in a speech he made there, made it clear that there was no limit to what the Negro people could take. "We will meet the capacity to inflict suffering with the capacity to endure suffering," he said. "We will say, do what you will to us but we will wear you down by our capacity to suffer."

By the time King made his speech the city merchants were hurting badly. Though the responsibility for defending segregation in their city had been thrust on them they noticed that they had not received strong support from the white community. Perhaps, they reflected, integration of counters would not be such a shock to their white customers after all. Weighing the known loss of their Negro trade against the possible loss of some of their white trade, they took a chance and notified the student spokesmen that they were ready to negotiate with them. The meetings produced an agreement between the merchants and the students calling for an initial opening of lunch counters to a few carefully selected Negroes who had been drilled in the techniques of nonviolence, to be followed two weeks later by the opening of counters to all who wished to sit at them.

At 3:15 on May 10, 1960, almost three months after the start of the city's sit-ins, small groups of Negroes quietly entered six downtown Nashville stores and sat at lunch counters for a mid-afternoon snack. Elaborate preparations had been made to cope with anticipated hostile white reactions; police stood nearby and a city community-relations group had posted churchwomen in the six stores to encourage the unsuspecting white people who would take part in this precedent-shattering experiment. One white church lady took her duty so seriously that when a Baptist minister came into the lunchroom where she was assigned, she asked him, "What are you doing here? This room is for Unitarians." By 4 P.M. the Negroes, the police and the churchwomen had left the counters. Nothing had happened.

The controlled desegregation went on until the end of May when all the city's Negroes were free to sit at the counters whenever they chose. If some of the white people disliked the new situation they made no outward sign of their displeasure. Lunch-counter sales hit their normal strides or increased. Store managers watching their customers cheerfully eating "mixed" wondered what all the fuss was about. On June 15th representatives of the Negro protest movement and of the city merchants met to hold an evaluation session. The merchants told the Negroes that sales in their stores were booming — in Nashville the ghost of a white boycott had been laid to rest.

Nashville's sit-in story had a happy ending and so did that of Atlanta, Georgia. "Atlanta's a city too busy to hate," proudly announced Mayor William B. Hartsfield after twelve months of sit-in demonstrations were ended by an agreement between students and merchants. The struggle had been long and hard-fought on both sides; White Citizens Council and Ku Klux Klan leaders from other states had streamed into Atlanta to bolster the forces of reaction there and they had been followed by the anti-Semitic groups that routinely move into areas of racial conflict. But Mayor Hartsfield's police force had been trained to uphold the law "regardless of race or personal feelings" and refused to allow the people's aroused passions to deteriorate into mob anarchy. "Atlanta does not cling to the past," Hartsfield said when it was all over. "People who swear on the old Southern traditions don't know what the hell they are. I think of boll weevils and hookworms. Robert E. Lee wouldn't even spit on the rabble rousers we have today. Think of living through this changing South — what a dynamic story! . . ."

But Nashville and Atlanta were only one side of the coin; on the other a combination of inflammatory statements by public officials and a segregationist press proved to be highly combustible material. In Montgomery, where white nerves were still frayed from the bus boycott in 1956, nine sit-in students were expelled from the state-supported Alabama State University and Governor John Patterson said the expulsions were necessary to prevent bloodshed and violence. "Once we give in to the threat of a mob," he said, "they'll get more arrogant every day." The mob in Montgomery turned out to be white, not black. When Ralph Abernathy led a group of 500 Negroes toward the State Capitol building where they planned to hold an anti-segregation prayer meeting, a crowd of angry white men rushed toward them. A posse of mounted sheriff's deputies arrived on the scene and, sirens screaming, a squad of fire engines roared up, but when the firemen connected their hoses to hydrants, they pointed them not at the menacing mob but at the peaceful Negroes. In Orangeburg, South Carolina, police forces actually turned fire hoses on orderly Negro students and in Tallahassee, Florida, tear gas was used to break up a demonstration. Many a Southern Negro in 1960 could echo Thoreau's words of more than a hundred years before: "They [the authorities] plainly did not know how to treat me, but behaved like persons who are underbred. . . . I saw that the State was half-witted, that it was timid as a lone woman with her silver spoons, and that it did not know its friends from its foes . . ."

Thus the sit-ins, put on in much the same manner throughout the South, met with varying responses. Geography, the local press and the attitude of public officials seemed to be the most important factors in determining the reactions of white communities to the sit-in challenge.

In the border states the combined moral and economic attack of the movement had its most potent effect. Weary of the inefficiencies, the lawlessness and economic losses that racial controversy brought in its train, many of the white men and women there were able to respond to the peaceful Negro protest, though often their response was reluctant and painfully slow. In several cities officials set up biracial committees to study the possibilities of gradual counter desegregation, and real progress was made toward a fairer treatment of Negro citizens.

It was a different story in the Deep South. There most white men were still in thrall to the past. There newspapers often deliberately heightened tension between the races by printing sensational stories about Negro crimes and "inferiority," and all too often public officials abetted a segregationist press by making flagrantly anti-Negro statements. Fear still played a large part in the lives of Negroes in the Deep South and though sit-ins were attempted there, they had less support from older Negroes than in the border states and they met with more brutal opposition.

And yet, though the sit-ins' successes were far from complete, they had an important effect on the average Southern Negro. He had seen that he need not wait, as he had waited in the past, for the white man to dole out freedom to him at a pace that the white man deemed proper. He saw that he could, without resorting to violence, effectively oppose the system that enslaved him.

It had all started in Montgomery. By staying off the buses and thereby refusing to cooperate in their own humiliation the city's Negroes had bumped up against a door marked "Freedom — White Only" and opened it a crack. With the sit-ins the Negro college student had pushed until he got his foot in the door. Now, breathing the fresh air that blew in from across the threshold, the Southern Negro was determined to get through to the other side. By mid-1961 there were many Americans outside the South who were ready to help him.

In accordance with the code of nonviolent resistance, Freedom Riders accept violent reactions to their protest without retaliating.

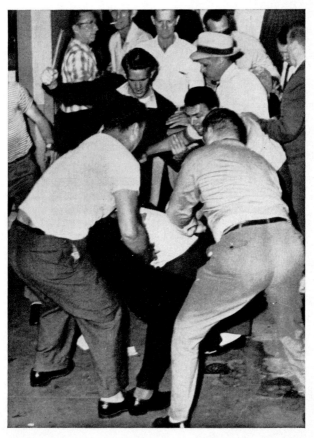

Over sixty demonstrators pray in front of the Albany, Georgia,
City Hall for a just verdict in a Freedom Rider trial.

8

The Freedom Rides
May 4–May 24, 1961

> . . . *Only through nonviolent*
> *demonstrations in which we accept*
> *violence without returning it in*
> *kind can we accomplish our pur-*
> *pose . . . The chances are that*
> *without people being hurt we can-*
> *not solve the problem.*
>
> — *Rev. James M. Lawson*
> *Nashville Christian*
> *Leadership Council*

I. *Washington to Birmingham, May 4–15*

TROUBLE, serious trouble, was brewing in the South and the
FBI knew it. On May 14, 1961, acting on a tip, the Bureau
notified police authorities in Birmingham, Alabama, to be on
the alert for violent mob action when buses carrying the
Freedom Riders arrived in that city.

On May 4th, seven Negro and six white members of CORE
had set out from Washington, D.C., on what they called a
"Freedom Ride" through the South. Riding Greyhound and
Trailways interstate buses in mixed groups, they ate "integrated" at terminal lunch counters and, in those terminals
where waiting rooms and rest rooms were designated as
"white" and "colored," several members of the group deliberately went into the "wrong" ones. Before they left
Washington, CORE had announced their Freedom Ride to
the press and had notified President Kennedy of the Free-

dom Riders' aims: they were out to test whether Negro Americans could use bus-terminal facilities without being subjected to segregation. In 1960 the Supreme Court had ruled such segregation in interstate bus terminals to be unconstitutional. CORE aimed to show the country whether or not the white South had accepted that decision.

On the first leg of their journey the Freedom Riders met only occasional pockets of resistance. In the bus depot at Danville, Virginia, a lunch-counter manager refused at first to serve them and then allowed himself to be persuaded; in Charlotte, North Carolina, a Negro Rider was arrested for trespass at a "white" shoeshine stand and was acquitted of the charge when his lawyer pleaded the Supreme Court ruling against segregation in bus terminals; in Rock Hill, South Carolina, prompt police action broke up an attack by white hoodlums on three Negro Riders.

The State of Georgia took the Freedom Riders in stride; in the cities of Athens and Augusta they were served at terminal counters without question, and in Atlanta, where lunch counters and schools had been desegregated the previous September, nobody noticed them at all. But uncertainty and foreboding hung over the CORE group. Alabama lay just ahead and Alabama was one of the Deep South states still presenting a solid front of "massive resistance" to integration in any form. No school in Alabama had yet complied with the 1954 Supreme Court order to desegregate; sit-in demonstrations in Alabama had been eminently unsuccessful and, as the Freedom Riders approached his state, Governor John Patterson had been quoted as saying, ". . . the people of Alabama are so enraged that I cannot guarantee protection for this bunch of agitators."

The FBI knew that violence awaited the Freedom Riders in Birmingham, and before they left Atlanta the Riders knew

it too. James Peck, a white member of the group, telephoned
ahead to the Reverend Fred Shuttlesworth, a Negro leader
in Birmingham, to tell him what time the Freedom Riders'
buses would arrive and Shuttlesworth warned Peck that a
mob of white supremacists was expected to mobilize at the
city's terminal. As the CORE group walked unnoticed
through the busy Atlanta bus depot, they found it hard to
believe that in another American city, only 360 miles away,
they would face danger at the hands of men who had never
seen them.

Violence erupted ahead of schedule. En route to Birmingham, the first of two buses carrying the CORE group was
surrounded by a crowd of hostile white people in the depot
at Anniston, Alabama. As the five Negro and four white
Freedom Riders sat frozen with fear in their seats, the jeering
cursing mob struck at the bus with iron bars, denting its
sides, shattering its windows and puncturing its tires. Police
authorities arrived and forced the whites away from the bus,
but when it lumbered out of the terminal and headed for
Birmingham, the Freedom Riders were uncomfortably aware
that an ominous caravan of private cars was following close
behind.

Six miles outside of Anniston one of the punctured bus
tires went flat and as the driver pulled over to the side of the
road the pursuing cars braked to a halt and their occupants,
spilling out on the road, ran toward the stalled bus. Suddenly
something hurtled through one of the broken windows and
landed sputtering and crackling on the floor. As the passengers watched in horror, little fingers of flame reached out and
fed on the seats and the whole bus filled with dense black
smoke. Though the mob outside tried to block the door, the
panic-filled passengers, choking and coughing, managed to
force their way out. Dazed and shaken, the Freedom Riders

stood there on the lonely road in front of their blazing bus and watched the white mob closing in. The attack was vicious but brief, for no sooner had it started than a squad of motorcycle police roared up to the scene and, firing pistols in the air, broke up the mob. Twelve of the passengers were taken to a hospital for treatment, mainly for burns and smoke inhalation. Later those of the Freedom Riders who had not been seriously injured proceeded to Birmingham in cars sent by the Reverend Mr. Shuttlesworth.

When the Trailways bus carrying the other four CORE members — two Negro, two white — arrived in the Anniston depot, its passengers heard about the violent mob action and the non-Freedom Riders hastily got off. Eight grim-faced white men who had been waiting in the terminal for the bus climbed aboard and the driver, obviously hoping to placate them, announced that he would go no farther until the two Negro passengers moved to rear seats. When the Negroes remained in their seats the eight white men moved forward and, kicking and slugging, forced all four of the Freedom Riders to the back of the bus. They then sat down in the forward seats and the bus pulled out of the terminal, headed for Birmingham. Later, James Peck reported that "for the entire two-hour ride the hoodlums craned their necks to stare at us with looks of hatred."

As their bus drove into the Birmingham terminal the apprehensive Freedom Riders saw that a large white mob had congregated outside the building and, in spite of the FBI warning, the city police were nowhere to be seen. The CORE group knew that they represented all those things most hated and feared by the extremist defenders of white supremacy who awaited them. Coming from the North they were "outsiders"; challenging the Southern way of life they were "agitators"; Negroes who demanded their legal rights were "uppity nigras" and the whites who encouraged them were the equally despised "nigger-lovers." Taking a deep breath the group left the bus. Charles Person, Negro, and James Peck, white, led the way into the "white" waiting room.

Person and Peck were immediately halted by several white men who grabbed them and pushed them into an alley-way outside the waiting room. There Person was surrounded by five white men and when one of them said "Hit him!" another slammed his fist into the colored man's face and Person fell to the ground, bleeding from the nose. He picked himself up and was immediately struck again. This time he fell back into the arms of the other hoodlums, who pushed him upright, and the white man hit him again. When Peck tried to help Person six white men fell on him, methodically punching him and beating him with pieces of lead pipe. Tom Langston of the *Birmingham Post-Herald* stood nearby taking pictures of the beatings and when the hoodlums saw what he was doing they attacked him too, beating him and smashing his camera. (But Langston had already removed the film from his camera and the next morning his paper printed his picture of Peck, bent over double, arms over his head, surrounded by kicking, slugging white men — a piece of lead pipe clearly visible in the upraised hand of one of the attackers.) The police had not yet appeared.

An eyewitness, Howard K. Smith, representing a national radio and television network, said that the attack was over by the time the police arrived, ten minutes after the bus had discharged its passengers. Smith said that by that time "the hoodlums had got into waiting cars and moved down the street a ways, where I watched them discussing the achievements of the day. That took place just under Police Commissioner Connors' window."

The injured Freedom Riders were taken to a hospital where doctors took fifty-three stitches to close the lacerations on Peck's face and head. The next day the two battered CORE groups assembled at the terminal and tried to get a bus for the next city on their itinerary, Montgomery, Alabama. But no driver was willing to transport such an explosive cargo. Advised by CORE headquarters in New York to abandon the Freedom Ride, the group left later that night by plane for New Orleans where the Negro protest movement had scheduled a rally for May 17th, to honor them.

Thus ended the CORE-planned and -sponsored Freedom Ride. A shocked and bewildered country noted that in the State of Alabama the loud clamor of white supremacists had effectively drowned out the voice of the highest court in the land; that nonviolent resistance to illegal segregation had provoked brutal mob violence and that local police authorities, whose job it was to control such mobs, had been tragically late in arriving.

The Freedom Ride, CORE announced, was over. But in Nashville, Tennessee a group of young people pored over the newspaper accounts of the riots and decided that the Ride must be continued. Thrilled by the courage of the CORE Freedom Riders, these young people, members of the Nashville Student Nonviolent Movement, excitedly agreed that they would take up the ride where it had been abandoned.

II. Birmingham to Montgomery, May 20th

Everywhere they turned the Nashville students ran into discouragement from their elders. They needed money for bus fares to New Orleans and they hoped that CORE would sponsor them, but when they called the organization's headquarters in New York, James Peck got on the phone and told them that it would be foolish to attempt a continuation of the Ride at that time. When the students approached the Nashville Christian Leadership Council, an affiliate of King's Southern Christian Leadership Council, they found that the older Negroes were less than enthusiastic about financing such a hazardous venture.

But caution and logic were lost in a flurry of youthful optimism and self-confidence. The students remembered that they had started their successful sit-ins and their follow-up stand-ins at segregated movie theaters without waiting for the blessing of older groups. They would go ahead just as soon as they rounded up the money they needed. An official of the Justice Department heard of their plans and tried to dissuade them. He spoke to one of their leaders, Diane Nash, and told her that it would be dangerous and irresponsible to undertake such a project while feeling was running so high in Alabama. "It was as if I were talking to a wall," he reported later. "She never listened to a word."

The students tried again to persuade the Christian Leadership Council to help them. They were so persistent that the older group finally relented and agreed to supply ten bus fares.

On Wednesday, May 17th, ten Negro and white students set out by bus for Birmingham, where they intended to start their Freedom Ride. By that time the public appearance of any integrated group was enough to send rumors of a new Freedom Ride racing over a thousand grapevines and it wasn't long before the Birmingham police knew they were coming. The bus was stopped on the outskirts of the city and boarded by several policemen. They ordered a white boy and a Negro boy who were sitting together to separate and when both boys refused to move they were taken off the bus in "protective custody." Two policemen rode the bus into the city and, seeing a crowd of hostile white people waiting in the terminal, they placed the other eight students in protective custody too.

Birmingham's Police Commissioner Connors didn't know what to do with the eight young people he was holding. Stung by a barrage of criticism for his failure to protect the earlier Freedom Riders, he was very anxious to forestall any further trouble. He had no grounds on which to hold the Nashville students but he knew that if he released them in Birmingham they might well spark a new riot. Hoping for an easy solution to his problem, he drove them under cover of darkness to the Tennessee-Alabama border, where he dumped them on the highway.

Commissioner Connors had not figured on the determination of young people who had sacrificed in the past to make nonviolent resistance work and who were willing and even anxious to face danger to make it work again. The boys and girls walked to a nearby Negro home, put in a call to their Nashville headquarters requesting that a car be sent to take them back to Birmingham and, while they waited for the car, devoured substantial breakfasts served to them by their hospitable hostess. The car arrived and as they rode over deserted back roads toward Birmingham, the tense and excited students listened to a local radio station reporting that though the exact whereabouts of the Freedom Riders were unknown, they were believed to be heading back to the city. Arriving unnoticed in Birmingham the group went directly to the Reverend Mr. Shuttlesworth's house where they met the two boys who had been taken off the bus earlier and then released, and another group of students who had arrived from Nashville in private cars.

In the meantime, in Washington, D.C., Attorney-General Robert Kennedy had been trying for several days to get in touch with Governor John Patterson of Alabama. When the Birmingham authorities had failed to act on the FBI warning, Kennedy had requested Patterson to see to it that buses traveling through his state were protected. Patterson had agreed at first and then changed his position. Since that time Kennedy was told that the Governor was "not available" each time he called. On Friday, May 19th, President John Kennedy tried to reach Patterson by telephone and he, too, was unsuccessful. Later that day, however, word reached Washington that Patterson would be willing to discuss the situation with a personal representative of the President. Accordingly, John Siegenthaler of the Justice Department flew to Montgomery, where he spent two hours that Friday evening with the Governor. Patterson assured Siegenthaler that the state of Alabama would be able to maintain law and order without any outside assistance.

While Siegenthaler and Patterson were conferring, the Nashville students, now numbering twenty-one, were in the Birmingham terminal trying to get a bus for Montgomery. They waited eighteen hours before they found a driver willing to take them. At 8:30 Saturday morning, May 20th, the exhausted boys and girls climbed on the bus and started for Montgomery.

As they sped through the Alabama countryside the Freedom Riders tried to relax and keep their minds off what might lie ahead, but the drone of a police helicopter circling overhead and screaming sirens of their motorcycle escort were effective reminders that theirs was no ordinary bus trip. Governor Patterson, it appeared, was determined to put teeth into his pledge to maintain order in the state. But, all at once, at the city limits of Montgomery, the police protection melted away. Suddenly feeling extremely exposed and vulnerable, the students did their best to keep up their spirits as the bus rolled over the remaining twenty miles to the heart of the city.

A crowd of about 200 white people milled around the bus as it came to a stop in the Montgomery terminal. When the students got off the bus, and newspaper and magazine reporters crowded around them, the mob closed in. The newsmen were attacked first and then the mob went after the Freedom Riders, kicking, pommeling and clubbing them with pieces of metal pipe. A few of the students tried to run away but they were quickly caught and thrown to the ground. A gang of white women assaulted two white girl Freedom Riders and flailed at them with pocketbooks and fists while men in the crowd shouted, "Hit 'em again!" When a white man tried to protect the two girls, men in the crowd clubbed him down, kicked him and left him lying bleeding and motionless. There were no policemen in the terminal.

John Siegenthaler had come to watch the arrival of the students' bus. When the wild melee broke out he tried to help one of the Freedom Rider girls to escape her pursuers only to be struck on the head and left unconscious on the ground. The time was 10:30, twelve hours after Governor Patterson had assured him of Alabama's ability to uphold the law unassisted.

Police forces arrived ten minutes after the attack had started, but the raging mob ignored them and continued to chase, club and stomp on the Freedom Riders. Everywhere there was wild disorder; the mob moved relentlessly first in one direction and then in another; screams and curses and shouts filled the air; the contents of the students' suitcases were spilled out and scattered on the ground; one of the Negro girls wept uncontrollably. At last, unable to gain control in any other way, the police lobbed tear-gas bombs into the crowd and the hoodlums, coughing and sputtering, gave up the chase and retreated, still menacingly grouped together.

An ambulance drew up to the depot but when the mob started to move toward it, the driver hastily pulled away. Siegenthaler lay for half an hour where he had fallen before he was taken to a hospital. When the mob finally broke up, those of the Freedom Riders who had not been seriously injured made their way to Ralph Abernathy's house.

Appalled by the new outbreak of violence and bloodshed, Attorney-General Kennedy tried several times to reach Governor Patterson and, failing, he dispatched a force of 600 federal marshals to Montgomery. His action was deeply resented by Patterson, but on Sunday evening reporters assigned to Montgomery unanimously agreed that only the presence of the marshals saved the city from an unprecedented disaster.

Martin Luther King, in Chicago for a speaking engagement on Saturday the 20th, the day of the attack, hurriedly cancelled the rest of his tour and flew to Montgomery to attend a mass meeting planned for Sunday night. He found the city in an uproar; ominous knots of people roamed the downtown section; sirens wailed as coveys of state troopers, city police and federal marshals sped through the streets in patrol cars and everywhere the air was thick with foreboding. A protective cordon was thrown around King on his arrival; as the symbol and spokesman of the Negro protest movement he was an obvious target for extremist fury. An impressive motorcade of federal marshals escorted him to Ralph Abernathy's First Baptist Church where the rally was to be held, prompting Governor Patterson to complain later that "it was just like the President coming to town." All through the day tension mounted as announcements of the

Negro mass meeting were broadcast periodically over local radio stations and cars filled with tight-lipped white men converged on the city from outlying areas.

As darkness fell, Negroes from all over Montgomery crowded into the First Baptist Church and on the surrounding streets groups of white men came together and talked in low voices. A squad of the federal marshals sent by the Attorney-General stood in front of the church and eyed the steadily growing white mob.

Inside the packed church approximately 1200 people rose to their feet and cheered jubilantly as Ralph Abernathy brought the Freedom Riders out onto the platform behind the pulpit. Martin Luther King addressed the meeting and said, ". . . the moment has come for a full-scale — non-violent — massive assault on the system of segregation in the South." His words were greeted by deafening shouts and applause.

The Negroes' cheers goaded the white mob into action. Bottles sailed through the air and shattered on the steep church steps and the sullen crowd began to move forward. The federal marshals stood alone between the advancing white men and the church, and one of them, realizing that the moment for decision was upon them, shouted, "If we're going to do it, let's do it!" and threw a tear-gas grenade into the onrushing crowd. The white men fell back but within minutes they had regrouped and let loose with a new barrage of bricks, rocks and paving stones.

Fear raced through the jam-packed pews of the church as the thud of rocks hitting the walls punctuated the sound of quavering voices raised in song. King was seriously worried; the thought of hundreds of Negroes trapped in the church by an enraged mob filled him with dread. While another minister stood in the pulpit pleading with the congregation to remain calm, King went to the church telephone and called Attorney-General Kennedy in Washington to ask for more protection. Kennedy told him that Patterson had seen the extreme peril of the situation and had declared martial law; National Guardsmen and city policemen had already been sent to reinforce the marshals. While Kennedy held the phone King went to a window to assess the scene and returned reassured. He told Kennedy that the Guardsmen had arrived and that it looked as though they, together with the marshals, would succeed in keeping the mob from rushing the church.

Slowly gaining control of the situation, the police authorities sent a message to the Negroes inside the church that it would be best for them to stay where they were until the crowd had dispersed. The weather was warm and the atmosphere in the packed church was hot and stifling. King and Abernathy walked up and down the aisles talking to the people and trying to cheer them. The beleaguered Negroes made themselves as comfortable as possible in the crowded pews; while some of them napped the others talked quietly as they waited for the signal to leave. The signal didn't come until six o'clock the following morning. When the weary Negroes filed out of the church they were escorted to their homes by details of the National Guard.

III. Montgomery to Jackson, May 24th

Governor Patterson was anxious to get rid of the Freedom Riders. When Martin Luther King announced on May 23rd that they would go on by bus from Montgomery to Jackson, Mississippi, Patterson said that he would not stand in the way of their leaving — he would, in fact, guarantee their safety as far as the Mississippi state line. Angrily disclaiming any responsibility for the violence in Montgomery, Patterson blamed it on the Freedom Riders themselves and on the federal marshals who, he said, encouraged them. And as for King, Patterson said, "the best thing for King to do is to get out of Alabama."

During the two days following the May 21st attack on the First Baptist Church, the Nashville students had been attending workshops in nonviolent techniques in preparation for the last leg of their Freedom Ride. These training sessions covered the subjects of the proper attitude of a nonviolent resister toward his opponent — respectful but firm; the ultimate aim of each Freedom Fighter — to peaceably force his opponent to give him the respect that is his due; and even went into such details as the correct posture for a Freedom Rider — erect, never slouched. During those two days the ranks of the Freedom Riders had been swollen by the addition of new volunteers; several leaders of the adult Nashville Christian Leadership Council and some of the original CORE Riders had hurried to Montgomery to join the Nashville students. When the whole group assembled in the Montgomery bus terminal on May 24th they numbered twenty-seven.

Governor Patterson was no longer depending on the discretion of Montgomery officials to preserve order in the city. State Guardsmen lined the streets around the bus depot while others kept watch on the roofs of buildings nearby. The Freedom Riders protested that they could not conduct a valid test of terminal facilities while bayonet-bearing soldiers dogged their footsteps, but their protests were to no avail; when they split up into two groups for the trip to Jackson, soldiers in combat dress followed them onto their buses, and as they traveled along the Alabama country roads state airplanes and helicopters hovered overhead while squads of highway patrol cars darted ahead and tagged close behind the buses.

The Freedom Riders had no illusions about the warmth of the reception awaiting them in Jackson. Mississippi was well known as "the state where no Negro ever protests anything" and Governor Ross Barnett had publicly advised "the agitators" to stay out of his state. The White Citizens Councils in Mississippi worked closely with influential politicians in formulating state policy, and because the Councils' aims emphasized the principle of states' rights and frowned on violent anti-Negro activity, they had strong support from the state's "better" people — the rich and the politically powerful. Thus, violent mob action against the Freedom Riders in Jackson was most unlikely, but a firm, undeviating insistence on "the Southern way of life" was certain. The Freedom Riders knew that if they tested the Jackson bus-terminal facilities the protection that Governor Barnett would offer them would undoubtedly involve a stay in the state's jails.

When the heavily guarded buses reached the state line, the Alabama convoy dropped behind and an equally grim-looking detail of Mississippi state patrols took over. At the Jackson city limits, escorts were again exchanged and the sirens of city motorcycle police heralded the Freedom Riders' approach to the bus terminal.

Emerging from their buses, the Freedom Riders were impressed by the length to which the Jackson authorities had gone "to prevent trouble." One Negro Rider, Frank Holloway, described the precautionary measures in this way:

> . . . a sort of tunnel of guards led from the bus to the "white" waiting room. In fact, they had blocked the way to the "Negro" waiting room, so that if some of us had changed our minds we couldn't have used the "Negro" rest room anyway.
>
> We got off the bus and walked through the "tunnel" of troopers, guardsmen, city police and reporters. At

the door of the waiting room a policeman stood there like the doorman of the Waldorf-Astoria and opened the door for us. There were more police inside. I guess the crooks in the city had a field day because all the Jackson police were at the bus station making tunnels and opening doors for us.

Once "tunneled" into the waiting room, the Freedom Riders were approached by a police captain who said, "You all have to move on." When the whole group remained where it was he asked politely, "You all going to move?" "No," said one of the Freedom Riders. "You all are under arrest," replied the captain.

In this way on May 24, 1961, twenty-seven Americans were arrested for insisting on rights which the Supreme Court had ruled were theirs as American citizens.

A wave of shame and revulsion swept the whole country as it read the story of mob violence that had come out of Alabama, but the white South refused to take all the blame. In effect it said to the rest of the nation:

We deeply regret the mob attacks on the Freedom Riders by our extreme segregationists and racists and we are shocked by the failure of our law-enforcement agencies to preserve the peace. However, the brutality and venom shown by the rioters are characteristic of such fringe groups as the Ku Klux Klan and cannot be taken as representative of the whole white South.

And we firmly believe that a large part of the fault lies with the Freedom Riders themselves. They are a new breed of the outsiders and agitators whom we are sure have always been at the root of our racial troubles. They deliberately set out to create a turmoil in order to dramatize their grievances and to rivet the country's attention on their cause. If they had not been attacked, their Ride would never have made the headlines — in fact, the success of their own nonviolent technique of protest depended on provoking violence from us. We believe that the desire to provoke violence is as bad as the violence itself.

Southern segregation is our business and we can cope with it alone. It has taken us a long time but now, in 1961, most of us concede that desegregation at some time in the future is inevitable. But we've got to move slowly. Northerners don't understand the South — they can't foresee the up-heaval that we know would follow desegregation forced on an unwilling South. We are beginning to respond to the sit-ins; they are our own Negroes and their protest is Southern-inspired and Southern-led. We deeply resent the Freedom Riders; they are outsiders who came looking for trouble. We can solve our segregation problems but we must be given time and we must be left alone.

Leaders of the anti-segregation movement pointed out that important changes in the *status quo* are never accomplished easily or quietly. Pledged to a peaceful approach and willing to absorb whatever violence might arise from their actions, they were confident of the morality of their methods. Defending the Freedom Riders, their answer to the white South could be put this way:

The United States can no longer afford the luxury of Southern segregation. The immorality and injustice of the system reflects on the country as a whole. Until America has set its own house in order it cannot possibly exert the moral leadership it has led the world to expect from it. Seg-

regation is every American's business. If turmoil is necessary to expose the evils of segregation, then turmoil there must be.

The sit-ins who, by contrast with the Freedom Riders, now seem almost respectable to you, were themselves often met with violence. We must push ahead with our nonviolent struggle for our rights whether or not our methods are acceptable to you. The Negro people will be satisfied with nothing less than full equality and they are not willing to wait all the years that the gradualists say are necessary.

Did the Freedom Rides present Negro leaders with the same problem that often plagued Mohandas Gandhi? More than once Gandhi took the lead in courses of action he considered too "radical" at the time because they were popular with the Indian people and because he was afraid that without his restraining influence their enthusiasm for protest might degenerate into violence. In 1961 it seemed that the Negro leadership in the United States was faced with a similar choice; they had either to sponsor the new nonviolent technique or to face the possibility that many of their followers would consider joining forces with the new Negro extremist group, the Black Muslims. The Muslims were ultra-segregationists: they aimed at an even greater separation of the Negro and white peoples than already prevailed in the South; they were demanding that a separate Black State be established on land to be given them by the American government — land that they said was owed to the Negro people as "back wages" for their unpaid labor during the days of slavery. The number of Black Muslims was still small but the organization offered a dangerous alternative to Negroes who became discouraged with the slow pace of nonviolent action. In any case, the SCLC came out in favor of the Freedom Rides and CORE resumed sponsorship of them; the outstanding NAACP lawyer, Thurgood Marshall, summed up his group's attitude to the new method of protest when he said, "The kids are serving notice on us that we're moving too slow . . ." and the NAACP took up the job of legal defense of the imprisoned Freedom Riders.

The questions of the validity of the Freedom Ride technique and of who had a right to demonstrate against Southern segregation remained unresolved, but it became increasingly clear that the Negro protest movement could not be stopped or slowed down.

How America had changed since Thoreau died nearly a hundred years before! Superhighways laced every part of the country and great cities relentlessly encroached on the forests and fields that Thoreau believed were the fount of truth and reality. Not content with his ability to fly from coast to coast in little more time than it took to get from Concord to Boston in Thoreau's time, modern man seemed more concerned than ever with hurry and bustle and the accumulation of material possessions. Yet 1961 found hundreds of Americans ready to sacrifice for what Thoreau called "Action from principle, the perception and performance of right . . ."

In the months that followed the original Freedom Rides, idealists in every part of the country turned to the new technique as a way of putting their principles into action. From Alaska, from Maine, from Florida, from New Mexico they came; ministers, teachers, housewives, office workers; whites and Negroes; Democrats and Republicans; sons and daughters of "first families"; sons and daughters of immigrants. Risking bodily injury and knowing that jail was almost a certainty, they interrupted the course of their lives and came south to ride the buses.

Giving his reason for coming all the way from Berkeley, California, to go on a Freedom Ride to Jackson, Mississippi, the Reverend Grant Muse said, "I have been preaching against sin and I think this [segregation] is it."

Shirley Smith, a white woman Freedom Rider from New York city said, "I saw no reason for not standing up to be counted at this precise moment in history."

The Chaplain of Yale University, the Reverend William Sloan Coffin, Jr., joined three white theology professors and three Negro students on a Freedom Ride because, he said, they hoped to prod "the sea of silent moderates in the South" into action.

In a Jackson city jail a Negro woman's cellmate asked her why she was there as a Freedom Rider and she replied, "So my children won't have to be."

There was no more violence, but neither was there any slackening of Mississippi's resistance to the Freedom Riders. As they walked into the "wrong" waiting rooms the new Riders were quietly and firmly arrested. During the six months following the first Freedom Ride, 315 Americans, in peaceable rebellion against laws they considered unjust, came to the city of Jackson to follow Henry Thoreau to jail.

"Minute corrections in the face of enormous evil" — this was what Martin Luther King called the progress made by the Negro protest movement in its first five years.

Some Americans, looking back over a hundred years of unrelieved segregation in the South, saw the results of non-violent resistance as nothing short of miraculous. Within eighteen months of the first sit-ins Negroes and whites were sitting together at lunch counters in more than 150 Southern cities; less than a year after the original Freedom Rides vigorous federal government action had forced almost every

Southern state to do away with segregation in travel facilities.

But, as King pointed out, only the surface of segregation had been scratched; nineteen million Americans had yet to attain first-class citizenship. The Negro people hoped that the sit-ins and the Freedom Rides would, besides securing their right to travel and eat "integrated," serve as distress signals to the nation, warnings that it must get down to the tedious business of eliminating segregation in the basic fields of employment opportunities, voting, housing and education. They knew that until colored men and women were given the chance to work at jobs that would challenge their skill and training, to vote unopposed in every part of the country, to come out of the social confinement of their ghettos and to see their children welcomed in public schools, they would remain a people apart, second-class.

When would a true desegregation of American society come about? The white South said, "Not in the foreseeable future." Negro leaders said, "Soon," and they insisted that theirs was the more realistic estimate. They knew that old prejudices and fears die hard; that resistance to change would continue until change was irretrievably accomplished; that, by their desperate nature, the last-ditch clutches at the past would be prone to violence. But they also knew that America was born of a struggle against injustice. They were sure that once their nonviolent assault on segregation opened American eyes to its evils, the national conscience would rise up and do battle with the past. They had no doubts about the outcome of that battle.

Conclusion

―――

THE STORY of the Peaceable Revolution has no beginning and no end . The concept of nonviolent resistance to evil is older than history and its application on a mass scale will be seen in tomorrow's headlines. It is one of those few great ideas that are the matchless gift from those who have lived to those who follow them.

Thoreau, rebelling against a society that would make him a party to injustice; Gandhi, leading a mass revolt against oppressive foreign rule; the American Negro, demanding the rights due to him as a citizen — white man, brown man, black man; living in different worlds, owing allegiance to different creeds and molded by different customs, yet bound closely together by courage and by faith in the goodness to be found in all men.

Thoreau was called an eccentric, Gandhi was considered a fanatic by many in his time, but today nonviolent resistance is widely recognized as an effective weapon in the hands of an otherwise powerless people when used against an opponent who cannot rest easy in the role of an oppressor.

Can the Peaceable Revolution be expanded in man's search for justice and peace? There are few today who would care to rely on nonviolence for the defense of their country against an aggressor or to trust its strength against an opponent notoriously untroubled by the demands of conscience. But such possibilities cannot be ruled out for the future. The power of nonviolence is abroad and growing in a world hard-pressed by the threat of final violence.

Suggested Books to Read

WALDEN
    Henry David Thoreau
ESSAY ON "CIVIL DISOBEDIENCE"
    Henry David Thoreau
THE HEART OF THOREAU'S JOURNALS
    edited by Odell Shepard
    (*Houghton Mifflin, Boston: 1927*)

GANDHI — HIS LIFE AND MESSAGE FOR THE WORLD
    Louis Fischer
    (*New American Library, New York [a Mentor Book]: 1954*)
TOWARD FREEDOM
    Jawaharlal Nehru
    (*John Day, New York: 1941*)
PRISON AND CHOCOLATE CAKE
    Nayantara Sahgal
    (*Knopf, New York: 1954*)

STRIDE TOWARD FREEDOM
    Martin Luther King
    (*Harper, New York: 1958*)
BLACK LIKE ME
    John Howard Griffin
    (*Houghton Mifflin, Boston: 1961*)
LET MY PEOPLE GO
    Albert Luthuli
    (*McGraw-Hill, New York: 1962*)

INDEX

The Peaceable Revolution

INDEX